PIANO • VOCAL • GUITAR

THE GREAT AMERICAN SONGBOOK

JAZZ

MUSIC AND LYRICS FOR 100 CLASSIC SONGS

Cover photos of Billie Holiday, Nat King Cole, Ella Fitzgerald
and Mel Torme courtesy of Photofest.

Cover photos of Louis Armstrong, Miles Davis
and Dave Brubeck by William "PoPsie" Randolph
www.PoPsiePhotos.com

ISBN 978-1-4768-7550-7

7777 W. BLUEMOUND RD. P.O. BOX 13819 MILWAUKEE, WI 53213

For all works contained herein:
Unauthorized copying, arranging, adapting, recording, Internet posting, public performance,
or other distribution of the printed music in this publication is an infringement of copyright.
Infringers are liable under the law.

Visit Hal Leonard Online at
www.halleonard.com

4	All Alone
8	All Blues
10	All or Nothing at All
20	Allen's Alley
26	Almost Like Being in Love
30	Alone Together
34	Along Came Betty
40	And the Angels Sing
17	Angel Eyes
44	As Time Goes By
48	Bernie's Tune
50	Between the Devil and the Deep Blue Sea
54	Billie's Bounce (Bill's Bounce)
64	Blue Moon
57	Bluesette
68	But Not for Me
78	Can't We Be Friends
73	Cherokee (Indian Love Song)
82	Comes Love
90	Crazy Rhythm
87	Cute
94	Dancing in the Dark
98	Darn That Dream
104	Days of Wine and Roses
106	Django
110	Embraceable You
101	Emily
114	Estate
118	Ev'ry Time We Say Goodbye
122	Fascinating Rhythm
127	Fly Me to the Moon (In Other Words)
130	A Foggy Day (In London Town)
134	Gee Baby, Ain't I Good to You
138	Giant Steps
142	Girl Talk
148	How About You?
145	How Deep Is the Ocean (How High Is the Sky)
152	How Long Has This Been Going On?
156	I Got Rhythm
160	I'll Remember April
164	If I Had You
168	In Your Own Sweet Way
176	It Had to Be You
182	Jumpin' at the Woodside
184	Just Friends
188	Just One of Those Things
194	Just Squeeze Me (But Don't Tease Me)
198	A Kiss to Build a Dream On
200	The Lamp Is Low
173	Laura

204	Li'l Darlin'
210	Love for Sale
216	Love Is Here to Stay
220	Love Walked In
207	Love You Madly
224	Lucky to Be Me
234	Lullaby in Rhythm
229	Lullaby of the Leaves
238	Mack the Knife
242	The Man I Love
246	Midnight Sun
251	The More I See You
254	My One and Only Love
257	Nice Work If You Can Get It
260	Night and Day
264	A Nightingale Sang in Berkeley Square
274	Nuages
276	Oh, Lady Be Good!
280	Oleo
284	On Green Dolphin Street
288	One O'Clock Jump
269	Over the Rainbow
290	Prelude to a Kiss
293	Reunion Blues
298	'Round Midnight
304	'S Wonderful
308	St. Thomas
312	The Shadow of Your Smile
316	Shiny Stockings
319	Someone to Watch Over Me
324	Spring Can Really Hang You Up the Most
330	Spring Is Here
334	Squeeze Me
337	Star Eyes
340	Stars Fell on Alabama
344	Street of Dreams
348	Summertime
352	Sweet Georgia Brown
356	Sweet Lorraine
360	Taking a Chance on Love
364	That's All
368	There Is No Greater Love
372	They Can't Take That Away from Me
376	Waltz for Debby
380	Watch What Happens
386	Wave
390	What Is This Thing Called Love?
394	When Your Lover Has Gone
383	Whisper Not
398	You Must Believe in Spring

ALL ALONE

Words and Music by
IRVING BERLIN

ALL BLUES

By MILES DAVIS

All or Nothing at All

Words by JACK LAWRENCE
Music by ARTHUR ALTMAN

Copyright © 1939 by Universal Music Corp.
Copyright renewed; extended term of Copyright deriving from Jack Lawrence and Arthur Altman assigned and effective June 20, 1995 to Range Road Music Inc.
Verse © 2000 by Range Road Music Inc.
International Copyright Secured   All Rights Reserved
Used by Permission

ALLEN'S ALLEY

By DENZIL DeCOSTA BEST

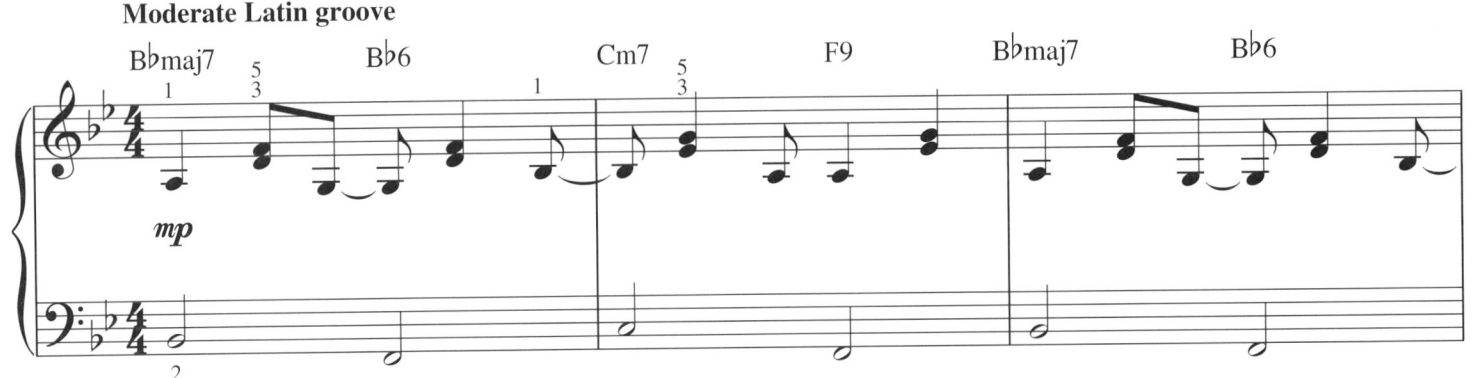

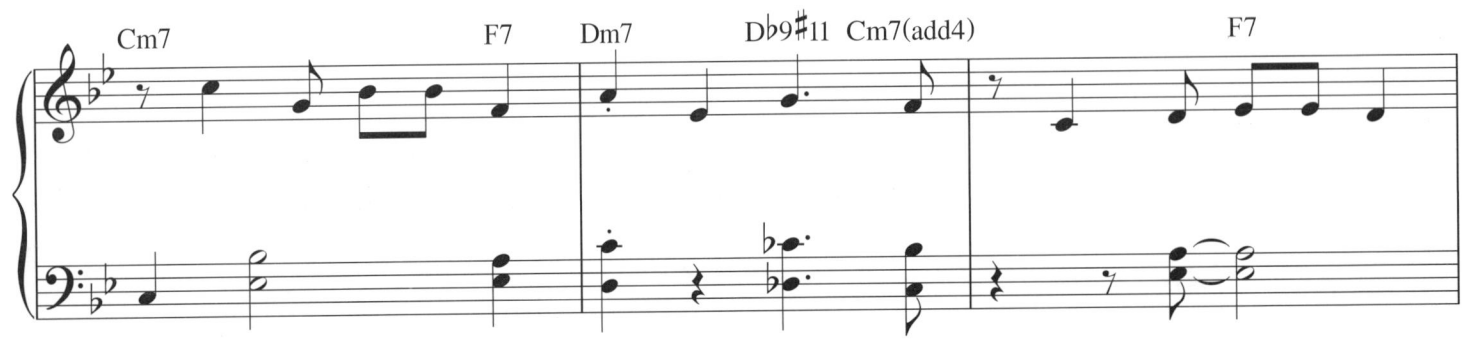

Copyright © 1949 (Renewed) by Embassy Music Corporation (BMI)
This arrangement Copyright © 2007 by Embassy Music Corporation (BMI)
International Copyright Secured   All Rights Reserved
Reprinted by Permission

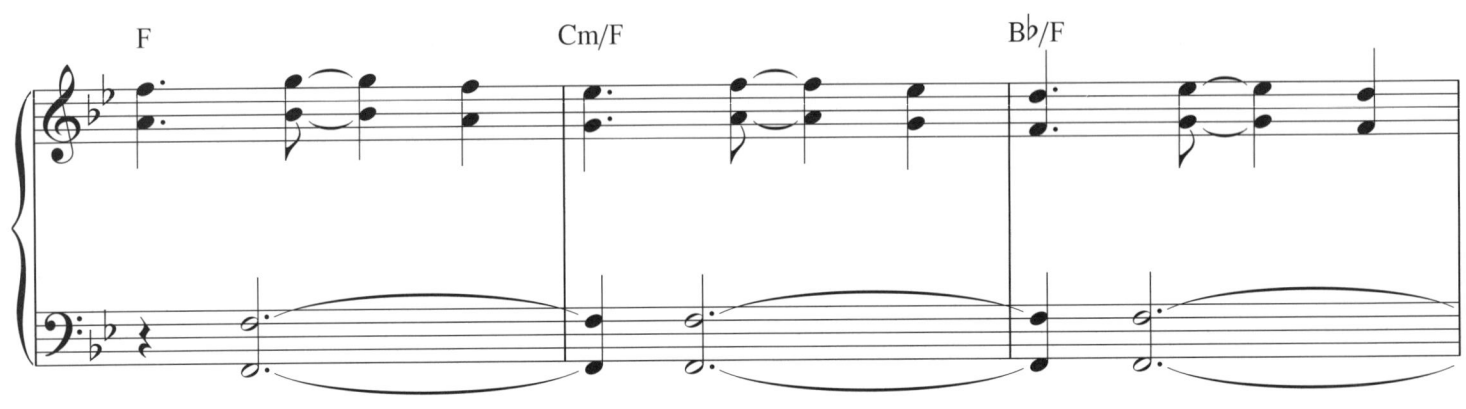

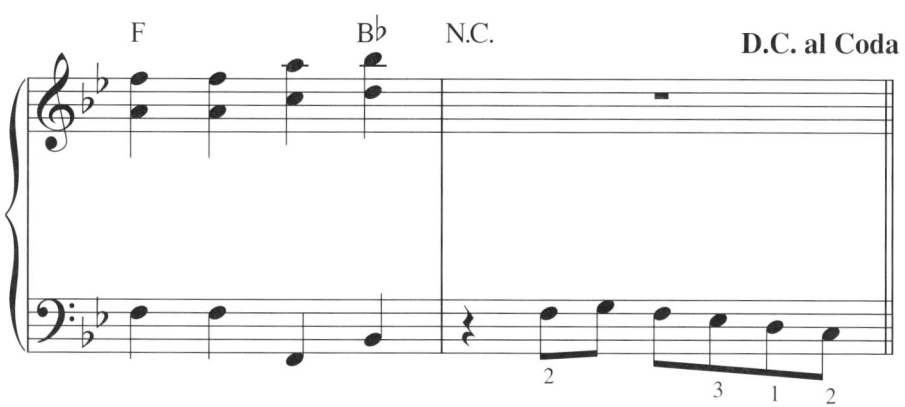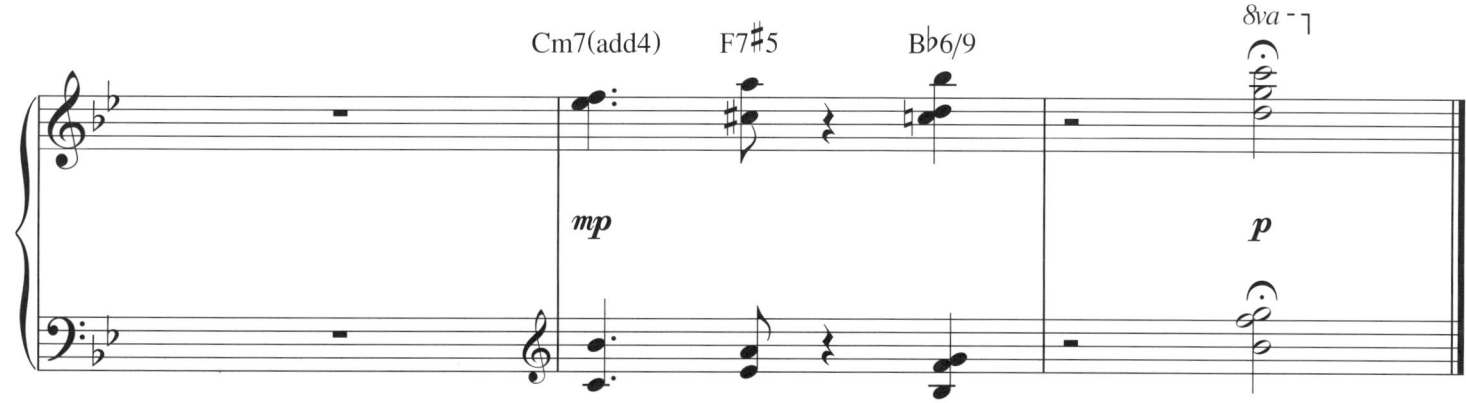

ALMOST LIKE BEING IN LOVE
from BRIGADOON

Lyrics by ALAN JAY LERNER
Music by FREDERICK LOEWE

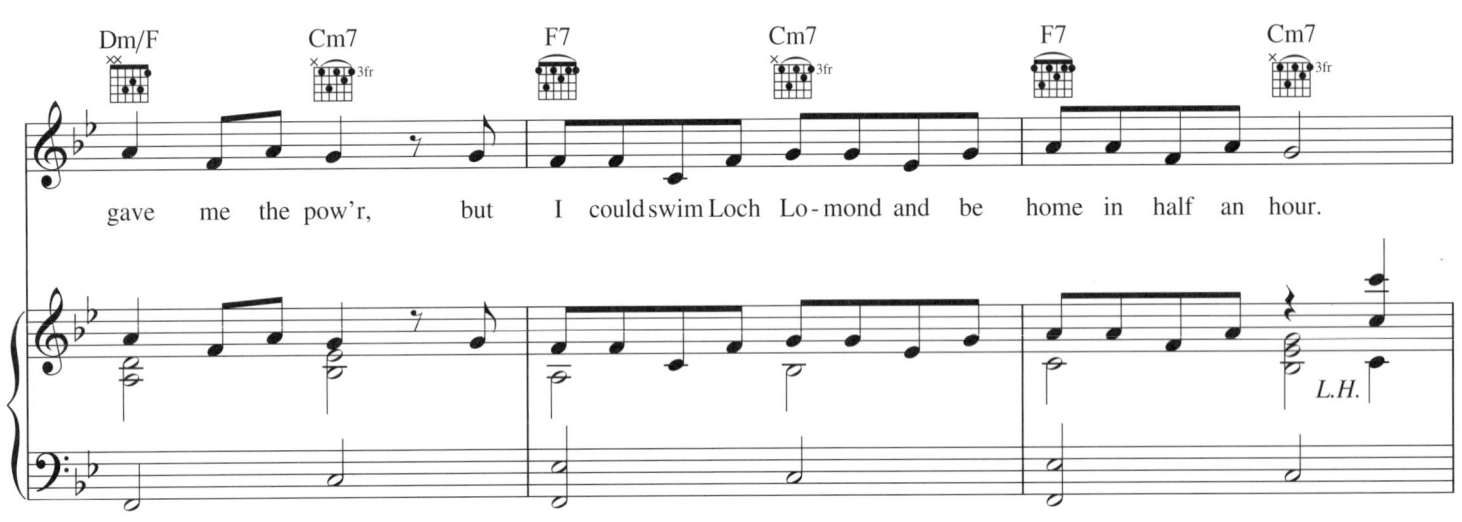

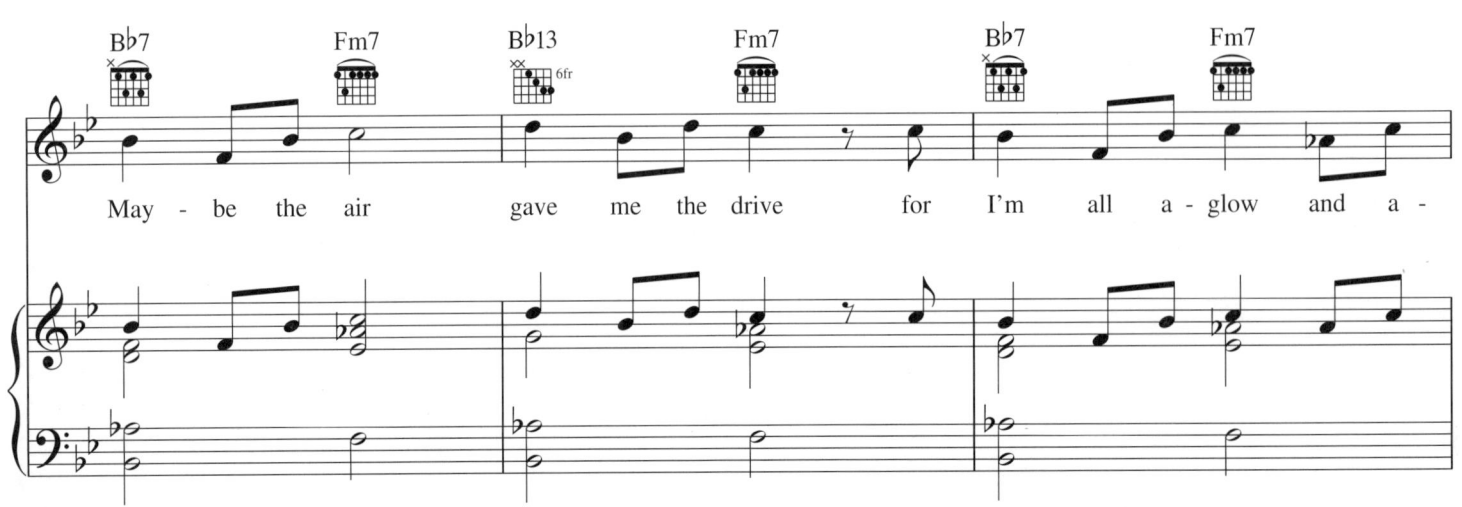

© 1947 (Renewed 1975) THE LERNER HEIRS PUBLISHING DESIGNEE and THE LOEWE FOUNDATION PUBLISHING DESIGNEE
All Rights Controlled and Administered by EMI APRIL MUSIC INC.
All Rights Reserved   International Copyright Secured   Used by Permission

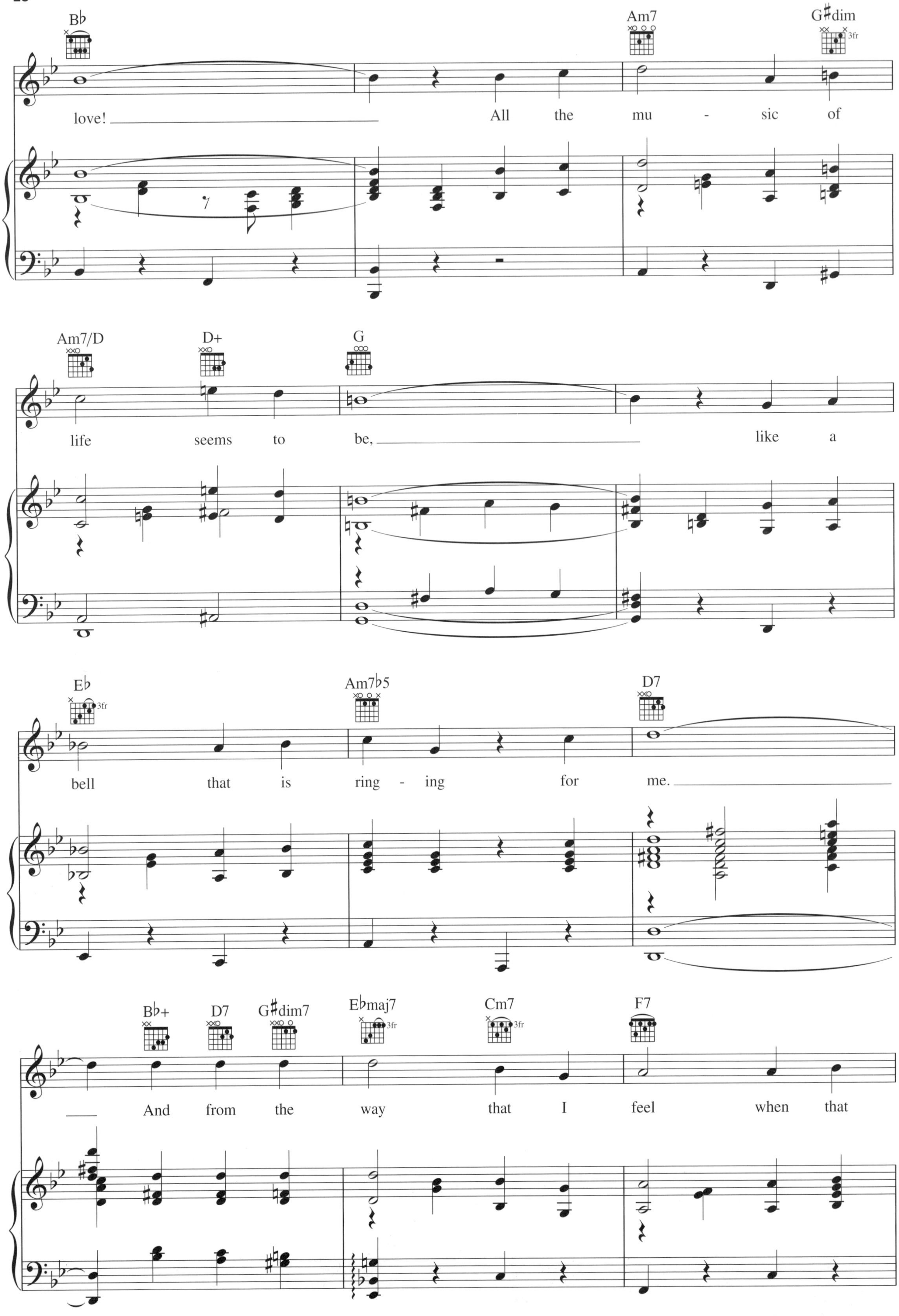
B♭
Am7
G♯dim
3fr
love!
All the mu - sic of
Am7/D
D+
G
life seems to be,
like a
E♭
3fr
Am7♭5
D7
bell that is ring - ing for me.
B♭+
D7
G♯dim7
E♭maj7
3fr
Cm7
3fr
F7
And from the way that I feel when that

ALONE TOGETHER

Lyrics by HOWARD DIETZ
Music by ARTHUR SCHWARTZ

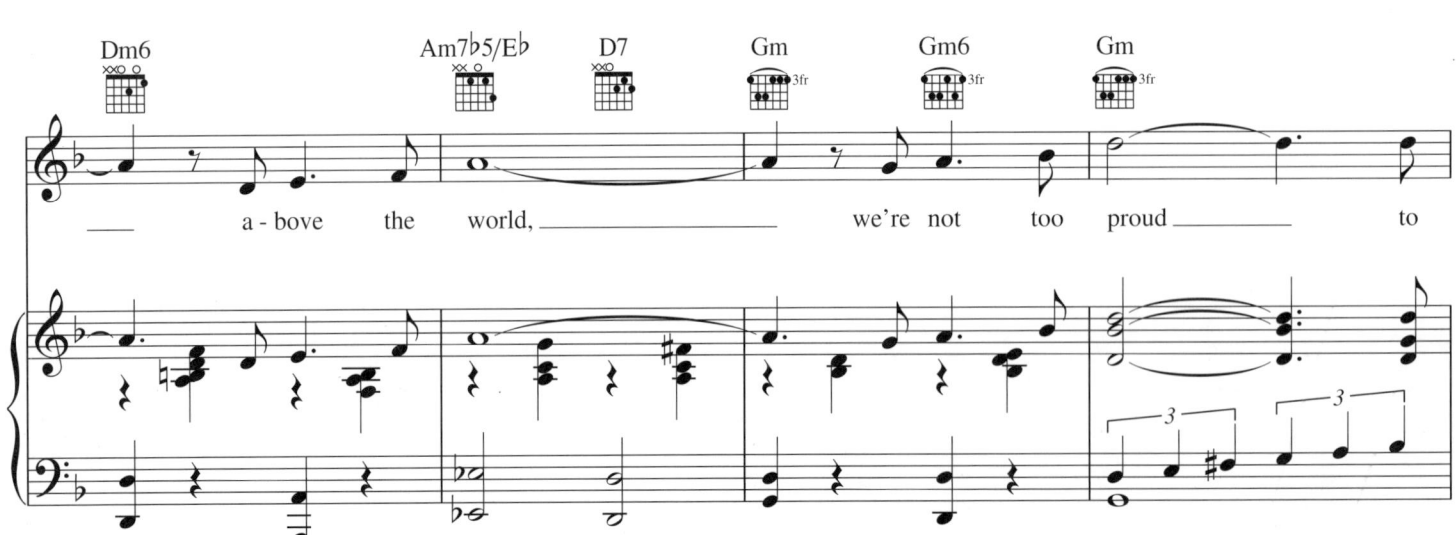

© 1932 (Renewed) WARNER BROS. INC. and ARTHUR SCHWARTZ MUSIC
All Rights Reserved   Used by Permission

ALONG CAME BETTY

By BENNY GOLSON

Copyright © 1958 (Renewed 1986) IBBOB MUSIC, INC. d/b/a TIME STEP MUSIC (ASCAP)
This arrangement Copyright © 2010 IBBOB MUSIC, INC. d/b/a TIME STEP MUSIC (ASCAP)
International Copyright Secured   All Rights Reserved

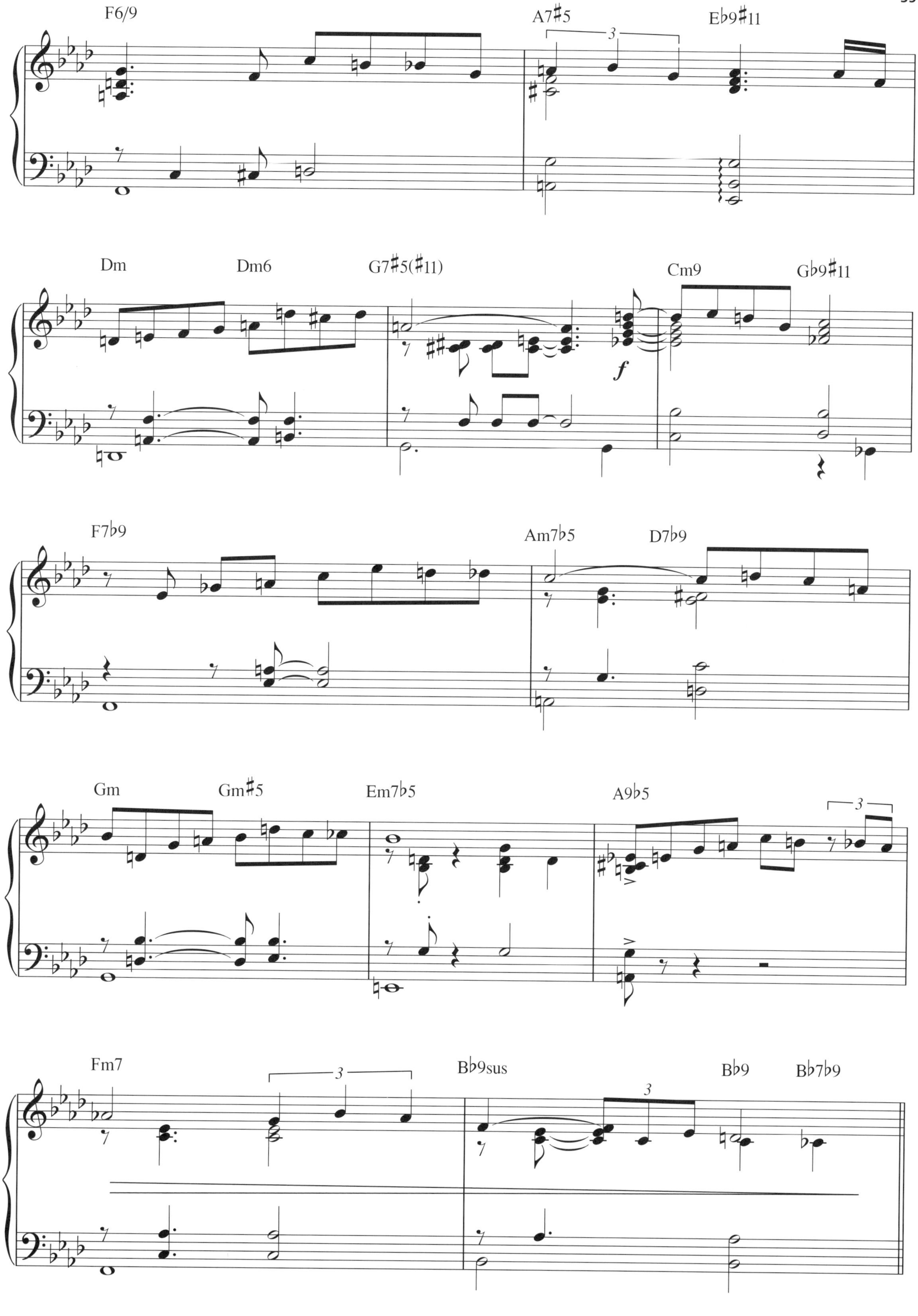
F6/9
A7♯5
Eb9♯11
Dm
Dm6
G7♯5(♯11)
Cm9
Gb9♯11
F7b9
Am7b5
D7b9
Gm
Gm♯5
Em7b5
A9b5
Fm7
Bb9sus
Bb9
Bb7b9

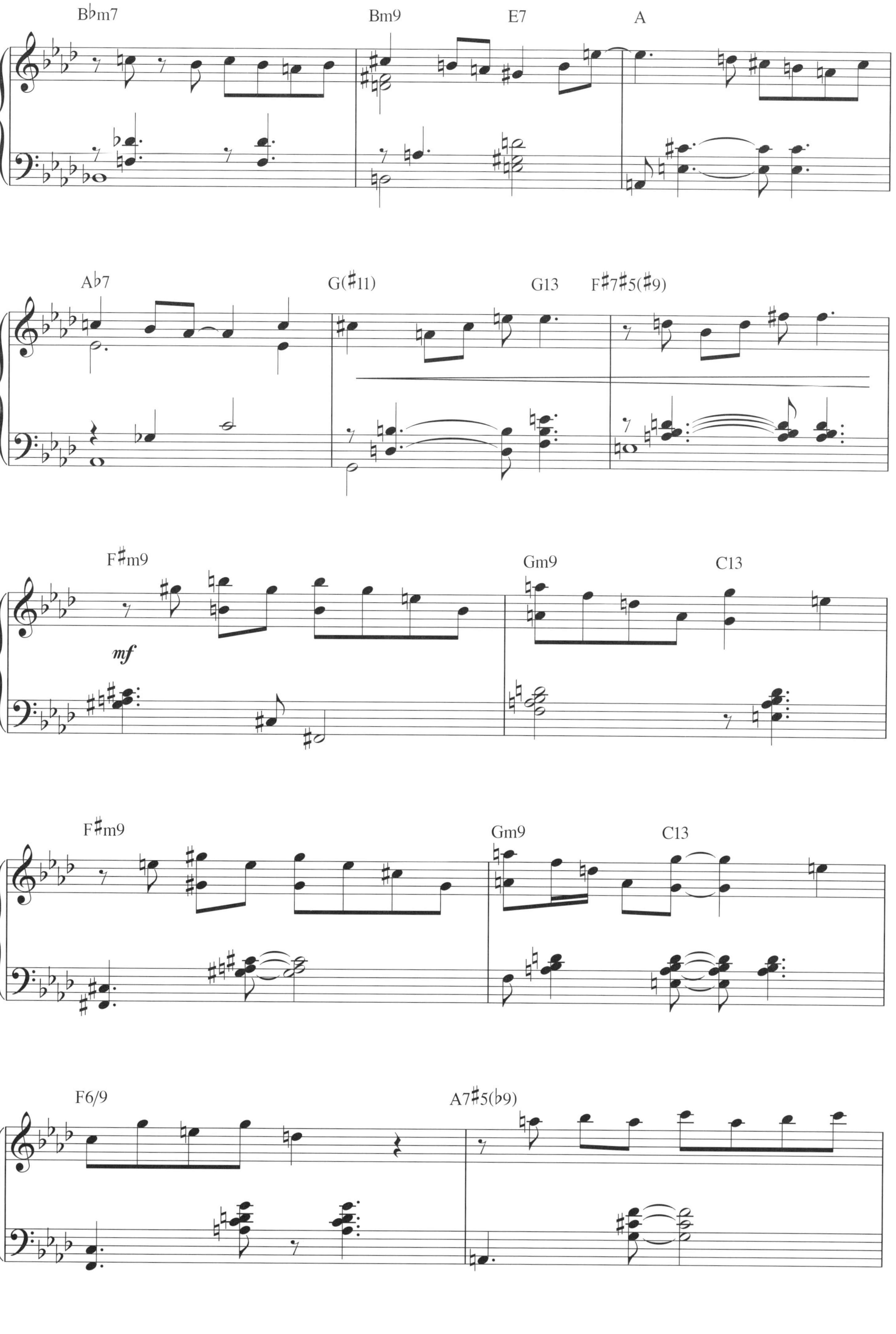
B♭m7
Bm9
E7
A
A♭7
G(♯11)
G13
F♯7♯5(♯9)
F♯m9
mf
Gm9
C13
F♯m9
Gm9
C13
F6/9
A7♯5(♭9)

Dm(maj9)
Dm9
G13
Cm11
C6/9
D♭6/9
C6/9
Cm11
B♭m11
F13♭9
f
Am11♭5
D7♭5♭9
Gm
3
Em7♭5
3
A13♭9
A7♯5
Fm9
3
B♭13♭9
B♭m7
mf
Bm9
E9/B

B♭m7
Bm9
E9/B
Cm7♭5
G♭13
F13
B♭m7♭5
E♭7♯9
3
A♭maj9
G♭9
3
Emaj13
Slower, deliberately
E♭7♯9
f
3
A♭6/9
8va
molto rit.

AND THE ANGELS SING

Lyrics by JOHNNY MERCER
Music by ZIGGY ELMAN

Moderately slow

We meet, _____ and the angels sing. _____ The angels sing the sweetest song I ever heard. _____ You

© 1939 (Renewed) WB MUSIC CORP. and THE JOHNNY MERCER FOUNDATION
All Rights Administered by WB MUSIC CORP.
All Rights Reserved   Used by Permission

speak, _____ and the an-gels sing, _____ or am I breath-ing mu-sic in-to ev-'ry word? _____

Sud-den-ly the set-ting is strange. _____ I can see wa-ter and moon-light beam-ing, sil-ver waves that break on some un-dis-cov-ered shore. Then sud-den-ly I see it all change, long winter nights with the can-dles gleam-ing. Through it all your face that I a-dore. You smile, and the an-gels sing. And though it's just a gen-tle

F7 B7 B♭7 E♭ Cm7 Fm7 B♭7♭9
murmur at the start, we
E♭ G7 Gdim
kiss, and the angels sing
F7 Fm B♭dim7 Fm C7 A♭m6 D♭7
and leave their music ringing in my
1 E♭ Cm7 Fm7 B♭7♭9
heart. We
2 E♭ A♭6 E♭6
heart.
rit.

AS TIME GOES BY
from CASABLANCA

Words and Music by
HERMAN HUPFELD

This day and age we're living in gives cause for apprehension, with speed and new invention and things like third dimension. Yet, we get a trifle weary with Mister Einstein's the'ry, so we must get down to earth, at times relax, relieve the tension. No

© 1931 (Renewed) WB MUSIC CORP.
All Rights Reserved   Used by Permission

matter what the prog-ress or what may yet be proved, the sim-ple facts of life are such they

Liltingly

can-not be re-moved. You must re-mem-ber this, a kiss is still a kiss, a

sigh is just a sigh; the fun-da-men-tal things ap-

ply, as time goes by. And

when two lov-ers woo, they still say, "I love you," on that you can re-ly;

no mat-ter what the fu-ture brings, as time goes by.

Moon-light and love songs

nev-er out of date, hearts full of pas-sion, jeal-ous-y and hate.

Wom-an needs man ___ and man must have his mate, that no one can de-ny. It's still the same old sto-ry, a fight for love and glo-ry, a case of do or die! The world will al-ways wel-come lov-ers, as time goes by. You by.

BERNIE'S TUNE

By BERNIE MILLER

B♭
Fm7
B♭7
Fm7
B♭7
Fm7
B♭7
A7
Dm7
A7
F
A7
E7
1
A7
G
Cm
3fr
A7
Dm7
Dm6
2
A7
G
Cm
3fr
A7
Dm6

BETWEEN THE DEVIL AND THE DEEP BLUE SEA

from RHYTHMANIA

Lyric by TED KOEHLER
Music by HAROLD ARLEN

(last time) Is there an-y-one a-round who can-not see it's the well-known run-a-round you're giv-ing me?

Copyright © 1931 (Renewed 1958) FRED AHLERT MUSIC GROUP, TED KOEHLER MUSIC CO. and S.A. MUSIC CO.
All Rights for FRED AHLERT MUSIC GROUP and TED KOEHLER MUSIC CO. Administered by BUG MUSIC, INC., a BMG CHRYSALIS COMPANY
All Rights Reserved   Used by Permission

Gm7 C7 F C7♯5 Gm7♭5 C7
I suppose you'll tell me I'm all wrong. It's a
8fr
F Fmaj7 F7 Dm B♭m
bit-ter pill to take, com-ing from you. Though I've made a big mis-take,
Gm7 C7 F Gm7 C7 F F♯7
what can I do? I don't know what makes me string a-long.
G7 C7♯5 F Gm7 C7 F
I don't want you, but I'd hate to
8fr

lose you. You've got me in be-tween the dev-il and the deep blue sea.

I for-give you 'cause I can't for-

get you. You've got me in be-tween the dev-il and the deep blue sea.

I ought to cross you off my list,

but when you come knock-ing at my door, ___ fate seems to give my heart a twist, ___ and I come run-ning back for more. ___ I should hate you, but I guess I love you. You've got me in be-tween ___ the dev-il and the deep blue sea. ___

BILLIE'S BOUNCE
(Bill's Bounce)

By CHARLIE PARKER

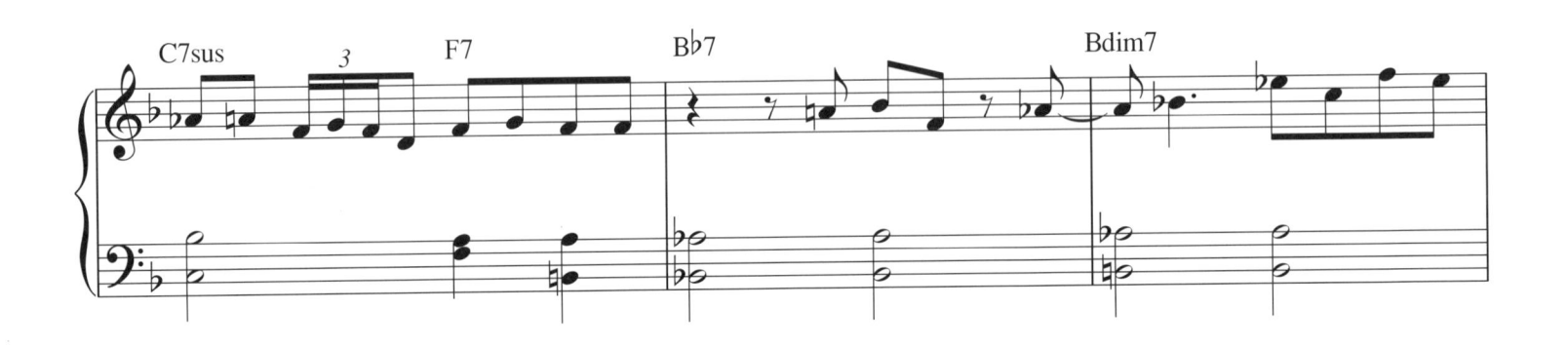

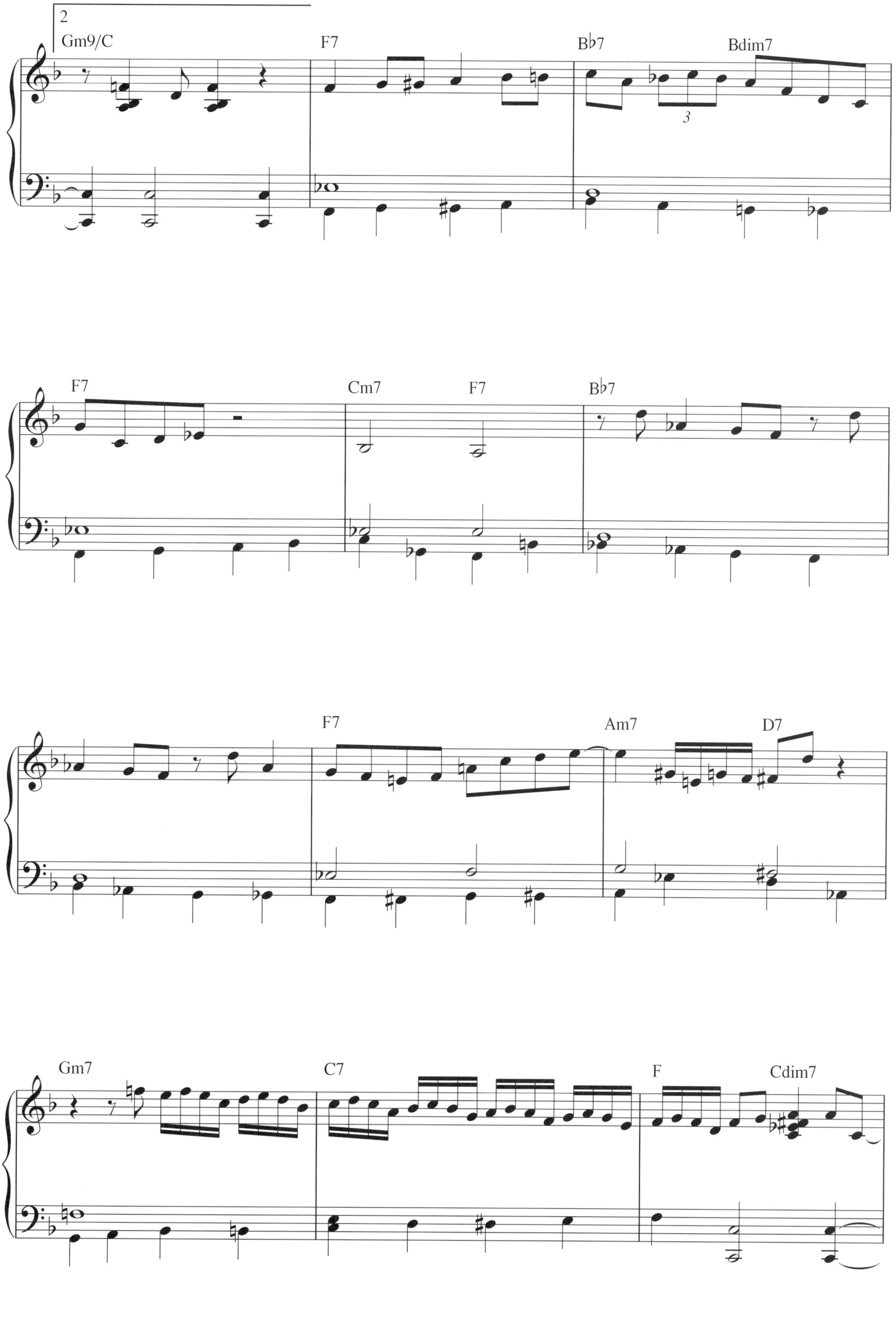
2
Gm9/C
F7
B♭7
Bdim7
3
F7
Cm7
F7
B♭7
F7
Am7
D7
Gm7
C7
F
Cdim7

C7sus
C7
F7
B♭7
Bdim7
F7
Cm7
F7
B♭7
F7
Am7
D7
Gm9
C7♯5
F/C
C7sus
C7
D.S. al Coda
CODA
F
D7♯9
Gm9
Gm9/C
F

BLUESETTE

Words by NORMAN GIMBEL
Music by JEAN THIELEMANS

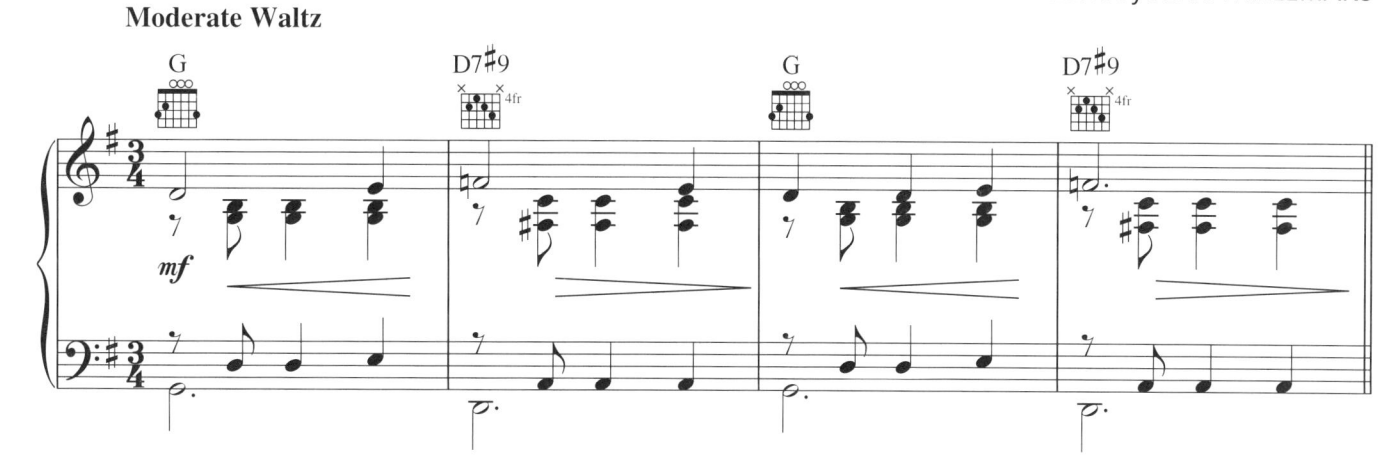

Moderate Waltz

Poor lit-tle, sad lit-tle blue Blues-ette.
Long as there's love in your blue heart Blues to share,

Don't you cry, don't you fret.
dear Blues-ette, don't de-spair.

Copyright © 1963, 1964 SONGS OF UNIVERSAL, INC.
Copyright Renewed; Words Renewed 1992 by NORMAN GIMBEL for the World and Assigned to
WORDS WEST LLC (P.O. Box 15187, Beverly Hills, CA 90209 USA)
All Rights Reserved   Used by Permission

You can bet one luck-y day, you'll wak-en
and your blues will be for-sak-en.
One luck-y day, love-ly love will come your way.

Some blue boy is long-ing, just like you, to
find a some-one to be true to.
Two lov-ing arms he can nes-tle in and stay.

Get set, Blues-ette, true love is com - ing.

Your trou - bled heart soon will be hum - ming.

Hum

Doo - ya, Doo - ya, Doo - ya, Doo - ya, Doo - ya, Doo - ya, Doo - oo - oo Blues-ette.

Pretty little Blues - ette mustn't be a mourner.

Have you heard the news yet? Love is 'round the corner.

Love wrapped in rain-bows and tied with pink rib-bon to make your next Spring-time your gold wed-ding ring time. So, dry your eyes. Don't-cha pout, don't-cha fret, good-y good times are com-ing, Blues-ette.

Long as there's love in your heart to share, dear Blues-ette, don't despair. Some blue boy is long-ing, just like you, to find a some-one to be true to.

One luck-y day, love-ly love will come your way. That mag-ic day may just be to-day. One luck-y day.

molto rit.

BLUE MOON

Music by RICHARD RODGERS
Lyrics by LORENZ HART

I went to sleep at ten. Life was a bitter cup for the
Hat-ing the morn-ing light. Now I a-wake in Heav-en and

sad-dest of all men.
all the world's all right.

Slowly, with feeling

Blue moon, you saw me stand-ing a-lone, With-out a dream in my heart, With-out a love of my own; Blue moon, you knew just what I was there for, you heard me saying a pray'r for someone I really could care for. And then there suddenly appeared before me The only one my arms will ever hold. I heard some-

A♭m D♭7 G♭ B♭/F Cm7/F F7
4fr 4fr 8fr
bod - y whis - per, "Please a - dore me" And when I looked, the moon had turned to
Fm7/B♭ B♭7 E♭ Cm Fm7 B♭7 E♭ Cm
3fr 3fr 3fr 3fr
gold! Blue moon! Now I'm no long - er a - lone
p
sim.
Fm7 B♭ E♭ Cm Fm7 Fm7/B♭
3fr 3fr
With - out a dream in my heart, With - out a love of my own.
1
E♭ A♭ E♭/G B♭7
3fr 4fr 3fr
Blue
2
E♭ A♭ E♭
3fr 4fr 3fr
mf

BUT NOT FOR ME
from GIRL CRAZY

Music and Lyrics by GEORGE GERSHWIN
and IRA GERSHWIN

Moderato

Old Man Sunshine, listen, you! Never tell me, "Dreams come true!" Just try it And I'll start a riot. Beatrice Fairfax,

© 1930 (Renewed) WB MUSIC CORP.
All Rights Reserved   Used by Permission

don't you dare Ever tell me he will care; I'm certain It's the final curtain. I never want to hear From any cheerful Polly-annas, Who tell you fate Supplies a mate; It's all ba - na - nas! They're writ - ing

Rather slow *(smoothly)*

songs of love, But not for me.
on a door, But not for me.

A luck - y star's a - bove, But not for
He'll plan a two by four, But not for

me. With love to lead the way
me. I know that love's a game;

A♭6
F♯dim7
E♭/G
Cm
I've found more clouds of gray Than an - y
I'm puz - zled, just the same. Was I the
F7♭5
Fm7
Fm7/E♭
Dm7♭5
F7♭5
Rus - sian play Could guar - an - tee.
moth or flame? I'm all at sea.
B♭7
E♭/B♭
B♭7
E♭
B♭7
E♭6
B♭7
E♭/B♭
B♭7
I was a fool to fall And get that
It all be - gan so well, But what an
E♭
B♭7
E♭/B♭
B♭7
F7
way; Heigh - ho! A - las! and al -
end! This is the time a fel -

-so, Lack - a - day! Al - though I
-ler needs a friend, When ev - 'ry

can't dis - miss The mem - 'ry of his kiss,
hap - py plot Ends with the mar - riage knot,

I guess he's not for
And there's no knot for

me.
He's knock - ing me.

CHEROKEE
(Indian Love Song)

Words and Music by
RAY NOBLE

Moderately bright Swing

Sweet In - dian maid - en, since first I met

you, I can't for-get you, Cher-o-kee sweet-heart. Child of the prai-rie, your love keeps call-

ing, my heart en-thrall-ing, Cher-o-kee. Dreams of sum-mer-time of lov-er-time gone

by ____ throng ____ my memory ____ so tenderly ____ and sigh. My sweet Indian maiden, one day I'll hold you, in my arms fold you, Cher-o-kee.

CAN'T WE BE FRIENDS?

Words by PAUL JAMES
Music by KAY SWIFT

Lyrics:

I took each word he said as gospel truth, the way a silly little child would. I can't excuse it on the grounds of youth, I was no babe in the wild wood. He didn't mean it,

G7 Gm7♭5 Fm Cmaj7♯5 C7♯5 F C A♭7
I should have seen it, now it's too late!
Tempo I
G7 C7 F6 D♭7
I thought I'd found the man of my dreams. Now it seems
I thought I knew the wheat from the chaff, what a laugh!
Dm7 D♭7 C7 N.C. G9 C7
this is how the sto - ry ends: he's goin' to turn me down and say,
This is how the sto - ry ends: I let him turn me down and say,
F B♭7 F Dm Dm7 G7
"Can't we be friends?" I thought for once it
"Can't we be friends?" I act - ed like a
3

couldn't go wrong, ___ not for long! I can see the way this
kid out of school, ___ what a fool! Now I see the way this

ends: he's goin' to turn me down ___ and say, "Can't we be friends?" ___
ends: I let him turn me down ___ and say, "Can't we be friends?" ___

Nev - er a - gain! ___ Through with
Why ___ should I care, ___ though he

love, ___ through with men! They play their game ___ with - out shame,___
gave ___ me the air? Why should I cry, ___ have a sigh, ___

E♭ E♭6 E♭7 D+ D D7 Dm(maj7) D G♭6 D9
— and who's to blame?
— and won - der why?
G7 C7 F6 D♭7
I thought I'd found a man I could trust, — what a bust!
I should have seen the sig - nal to stop, — what a flop!
Dm7 D♭7 C7 N.C. G9 C7
This is how the sto - ry ends: he's goin' to turn me down — and say,
This is how the sto - ry ends: I let him turn me down — and say,
F B♭7 F
"Can't we be friends?" —
"Can't we be friends?" —
1 F6 C A♭7
2 F6 F
3fr
4fr
9fr

COMES LOVE

Words and Music by LEW BROWN, CHARLIE TOBIAS and SAM STEPT

Moderately

Where there's a will there's a way, An-y-thing can be done to-day. Did I say an-y-thing? That's my mis-take. Tho'

© 1939 (Renewed) WB MUSIC CORP., CHAPPELL & CO. and CHED MUSIC CORPORATION
All Rights for CHED MUSIC CORPORATION Administered by WB MUSIC CORP.
All Rights Reserved   Used by Permission

you have the pow'r of a Bo-na-parte To save your soul you can't save your heart, When that Cu-pid guy won't give you a break. Comes a

rain storm   Put your rubbers on your feet, Comes a snow-storm   You can
heat wave   You can hurry to the shore, Comes a summons   You can

get a little heat; Comes love, _____ nothing can be
hide behind the door; Comes love, _____ nothing can be

done. _____ Comes a fire _____ Then you
done. _____ Comes the measles   You can

know just what to do, Blow a tire _____ You can
quarantine the room. Comes a "Mousie"   You can

C G♯dim7 D7 E♭7 D7
buy an - oth - er shoe; Comes love, nothing - ing can be
chase it with a broom; Comes love, nothing - ing can be
Gm Gm6 D7 G7
done. Don't try
done. That's all,
Cm G7 Cm G7 Cm
hid - in' 'Cause there is - n't an - y use,
broth - er, if you've ev - er been in love,
F7 D7
You'll start slid - in' When your heart turns on
That's all, broth - er! You know what I'm speak -
3fr

the juice.__ Comes a head-ache You can lose it in a day, Comes a
-ing of!__ Comes a night-mare You can al-ways stay a-wake, Comes de-

tooth-ache See your den-tist right a-way; Comes
pres-sion You may get an-oth-er break; Comes

love,_____ noth-ing can be done!_____
love,_____ noth-ing can be

Comes a done!_____

CUTE

Music by NEAL HEFTI
Lyrics by STANLEY STYNE

Those big blue eyes, — that turned-up nose, —
But in your case — a classic face, —
that cool and carefree pose. —
I may regret this yet! —
I mean I like your style. —
I like — the things you say, —

That sly in-trigu-ing smile, your most per-sua-sive way.

your ev-'ry mood, your at-ti-tude,
My state of mind is re-de-signed,

just add up to you're cute!
be-cause I find you're cute!

CRAZY RHYTHM
from THE COTTON CLUB

Words by IRVING CAESAR
Music by JOSEPH MEYER and ROGER WOLFE KAHN

Moderately

I feel like the Em-per-or Ne-ro when Rome was a ver-y hot town;
Ev-'ry Greek, each Turk and each La-tin, the Rus-sians and Prus-sians as well,

Fa-ther Knick-er-bock-er, for-give me, I play while your cit-y burns down;
when they seek the lure of Man-hat-tan, are sure to come un-der your spell.

Through all its night life I
Their na-tive folks songs they

Copyright © 1928 (Renewed) JoRo Music Corporation, New York, NY Irving Caesar Music and WB Music Corp.
All Rights on behalf of Irving Caesar Music Administered by WB Music Corp.
International Copyright Secured All Rights Reserved

fid - dle a - way, ___ it's not the right life, but think of the pay. ___
soon throw a - way, ___ those Har - lem smoke songs, they soon learn to play. ___

Some day I will bid it good-bye, ___ I'll put my fid - dle a - way ___ and I'll say:
Can't you fall for Car - ne - gie Hall; ___ oh, Dan - ny, call it a day ___ and we'll say:

Cra - zy rhy - thm, here's the door - way, I'll go my way,

you'll go your ___ way, cra - zy rhy - thm, from now on ___ we're

G6 G Gmaj7 G6 Gmaj7 G6
through. Here is where we have a show - down,
Gmaj7 G6 Gmaj7 G6 D7 Am7
I'm too high - hat, you're too low - down, cra - zy rhy - thm,
D7 Am7 D7 G6 D7
here's good - bye to you. They say that
G7 Dm7 G7 Dm7 G7 C G7 C
when a high - brow meets a low - brow walk - ing a - long Broad - way,

soon the high-brow, he has no brow, ain't it a shame, and you're to blame. What's the use of Pro-hi-bi-tion? You pro-duce the same con-di-tion, cra-zy rhy-thm, I've gone cra-zy, too.

too.

DANCING IN THE DARK

from THE BAND WAGON
from DANCING IN THE DARK

Words by HOWARD DIETZ
Music by ARTHUR SCHWARTZ

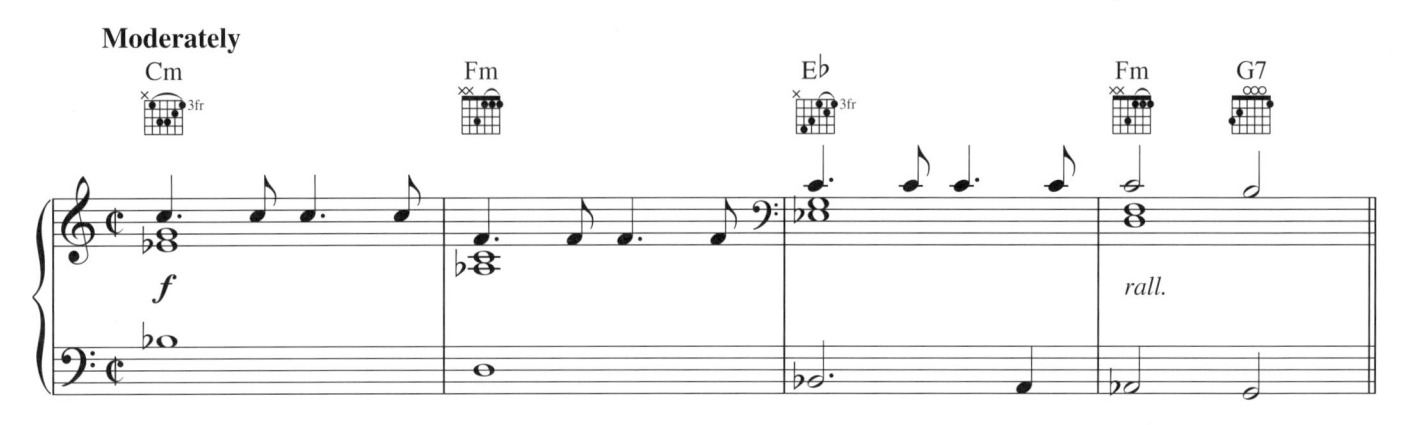

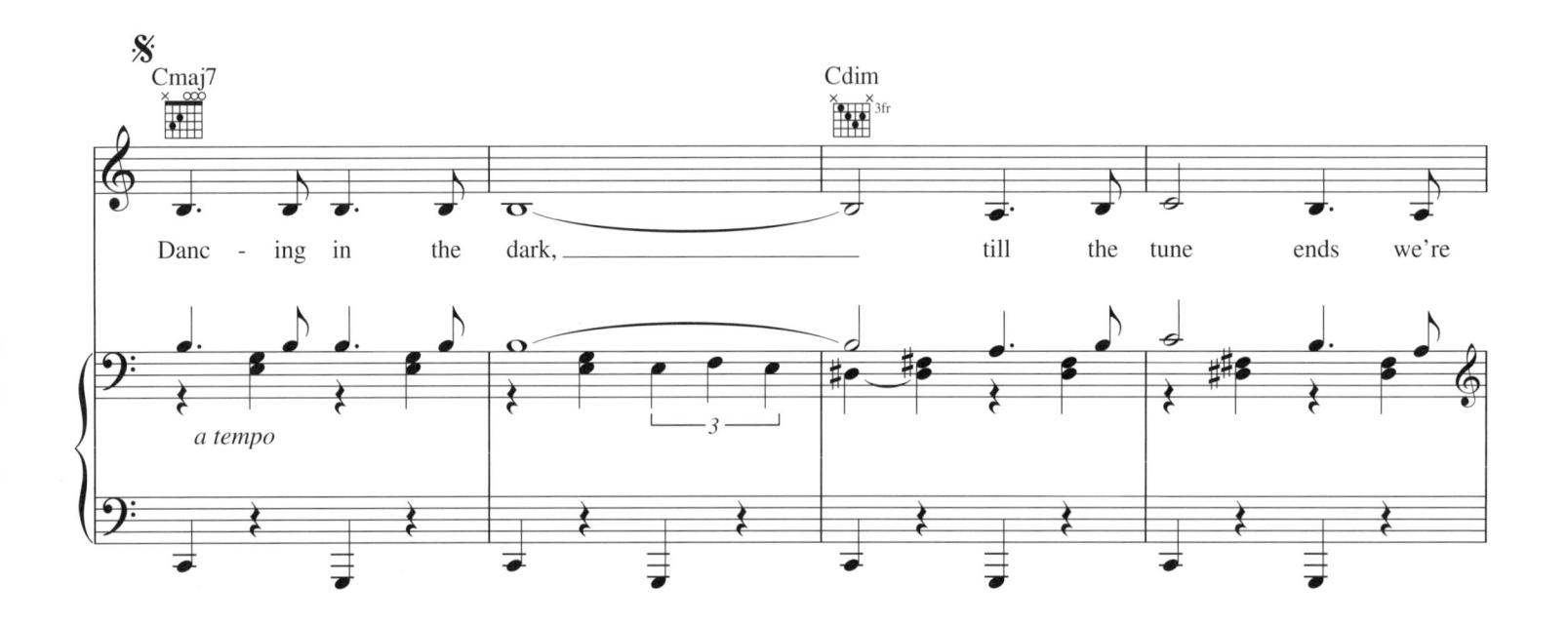

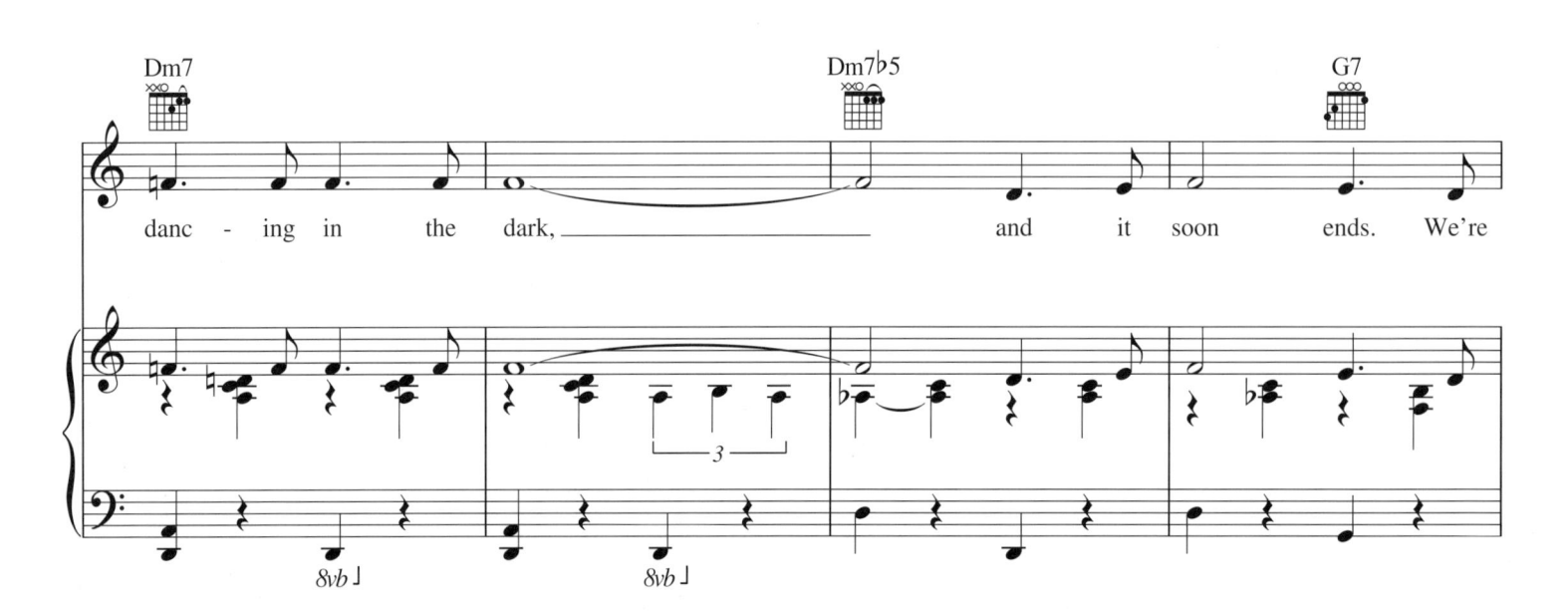

Danc-ing in the dark, _____ till the tune ends we're danc-ing in the dark, _____ and it soon ends. We're

© 1931 (Renewed) WARNER BROS. INC. and ARTHUR SCHWARTZ PUB. DES.
All Rights Reserved   Used by Permission

waltz - ing in the won - der of why we're here.

Time hur - ries by, we're here and gone,

look - ing for the light of a new love to

bright - en up the night. I have you, love, and

we can face the mu-sic to-geth-er,

danc-ing in the dark.

What though love is old?

What though song is old? Through them

we can be young! _____ Hear this heart of mine make yours part of mine! Dear one, tell me that we're one! dark.

DARN THAT DREAM

Lyric by EDDIE DE LANGE
Music by JIMMY VAN HEUSEN

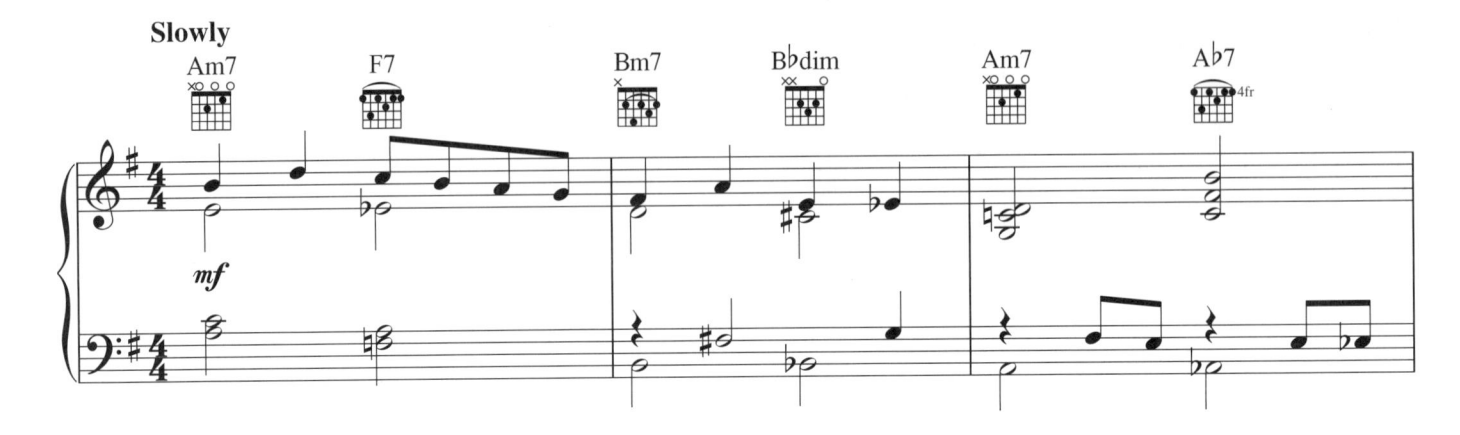

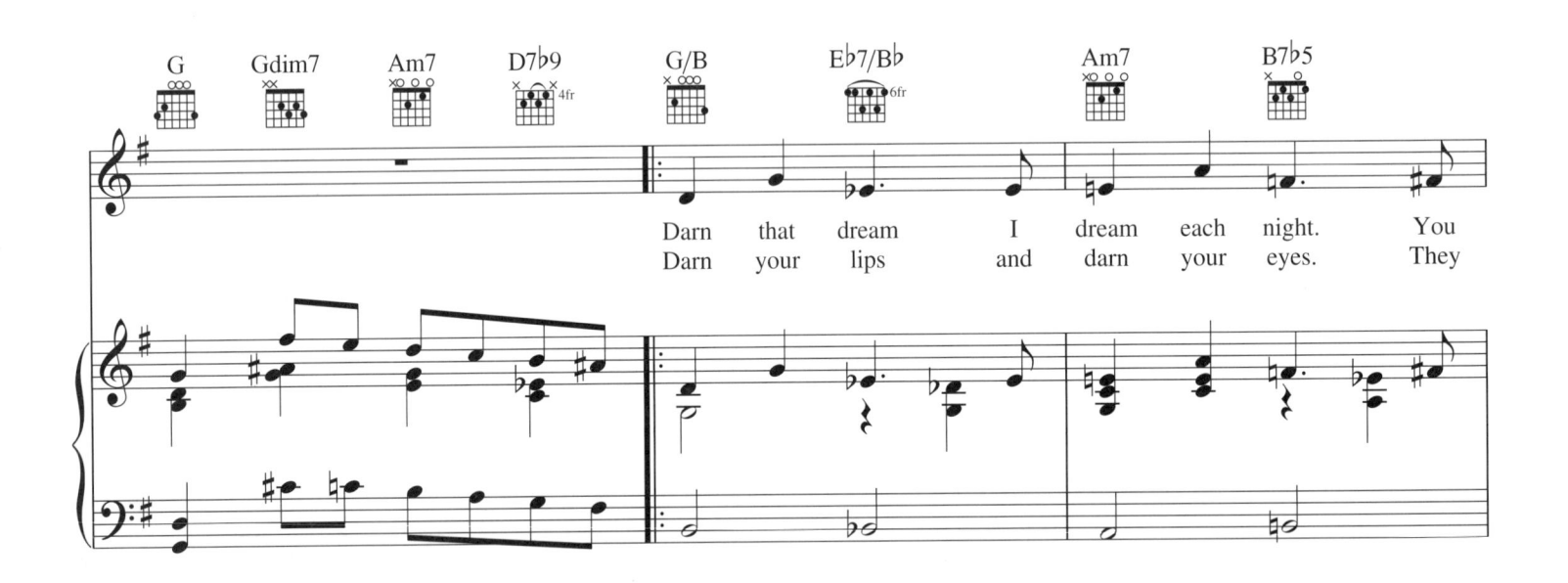

Darn that dream I dream each night. You
Darn your lips and darn your eyes. They

say you love me and you hold me tight, but when I a-wake you're
lift me high a-bove the moon-lit skies, then I tum-ble out of

1
Bm7 B♭dim Am7 A♭7 G Cm/G Am D7♯5
out of sight, oh, darn that dream.
Par - a - dise, oh,
2
Am7 A♭7 G B♭7 E♭ Cm
darn that dream. Darn that one - track
Fm7 B♭7 B♭7♯5 E♭/G G♭dim
mind of mine, it can't un - der - stand that
Fm7 B♭9 B♭7♭9 E♭ Cm Gm Gm(maj7) Gm7 Gm6
you don't care. Just to change that mood I'm in, I'd

Am7 D7 E♭7 D7 G/B E♭7/B♭
6fr
wel-come a nice old night - mare. Darn that dream and
Am7 B7♭5 Em Em(maj7) Ddim7 C
bless it, too. With - out that dream, I nev - er
Bm7♭5 E9 Am7 F7
would have you. But it haunts me and it
Bm7 B♭dim Am7 A♭7 G F♯7 G6/9
4fr
won't come true, oh, darn that dream.

EMILY
from the MGM Motion Picture THE AMERICANIZATION OF EMILY

Music by JOHNNY MANDEL
Words by JOHNNY MERCER

Moderately slow

Em-i-ly, Em-i-ly, Em-i-ly has the mur-mur-ing sound of May. All sil-ver bells, cor-al shells, car-ou-sels and the

© 1964 METRO-GOLDWYN-MAYER, INC.
Copyright Renewed 1992 EMI Miller Catalog, INC.
Exclusive Print Rights Administered by ALFRED MUSIC
All Rights Reserved Used by Permission

laugh-ter of chil-dren at play say.

Em-i-ly, Em-i-ly, Em-i-ly and we

fade to a mar-vel-ous view, Two

lov-ers a-lone and out of sight seeing

im-a-ges _____ in the fire-light. _____ As my eyes vis-ual-ize a fam-i-ly, _____ they see dream-i-ly, Em-i-ly too. _____

too. _____

rit. e dim.

DAYS OF WINE AND ROSES

from DAYS OF WINE AND ROSES

Lyric by JOHNNY MERCER
Music by HENRY MANCINI

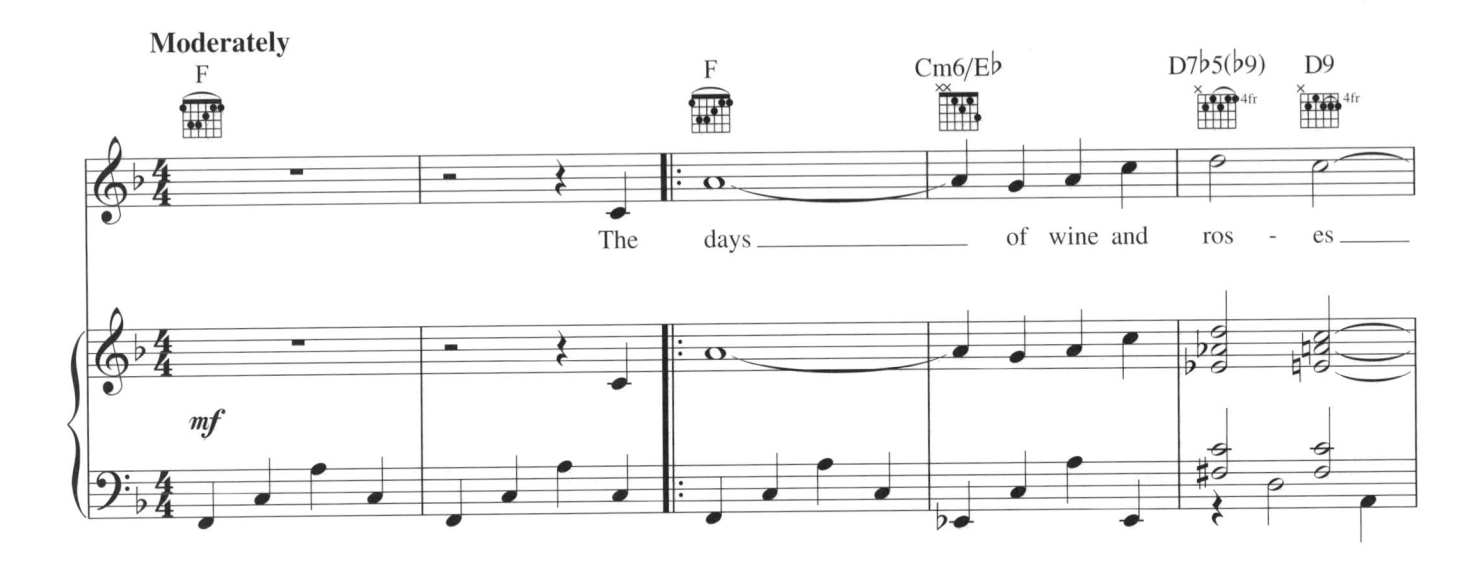

Moderately

The days of wine and ros-es laugh and run a-way like a child at play, through the mead-ow-land to-ward a clos-ing door, a door marked "Nev-er-more," that

© 1962 (Renewed) WB MUSIC CORP. and THE JOHNNY MERCER FOUNDATION
All Rights Administered by WB MUSIC CORP.
All Rights Reserved   Used by Permission

wasn't there before. The lonely night dis-closes just a passing breeze filled with memories of the golden smile that introduced me to the days of wine and roses and you. The you.

DJANGO

By JOHN LEWIS

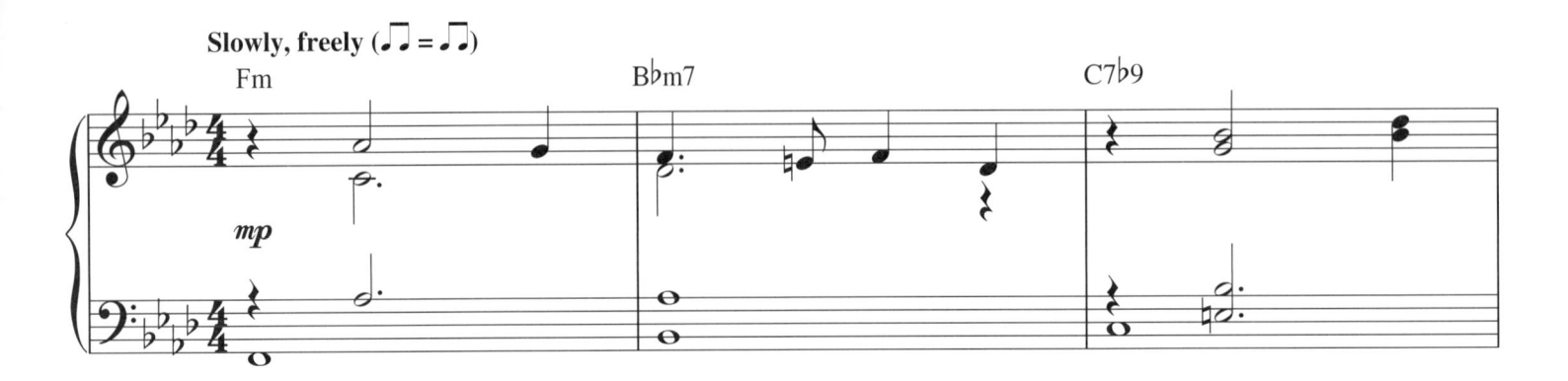

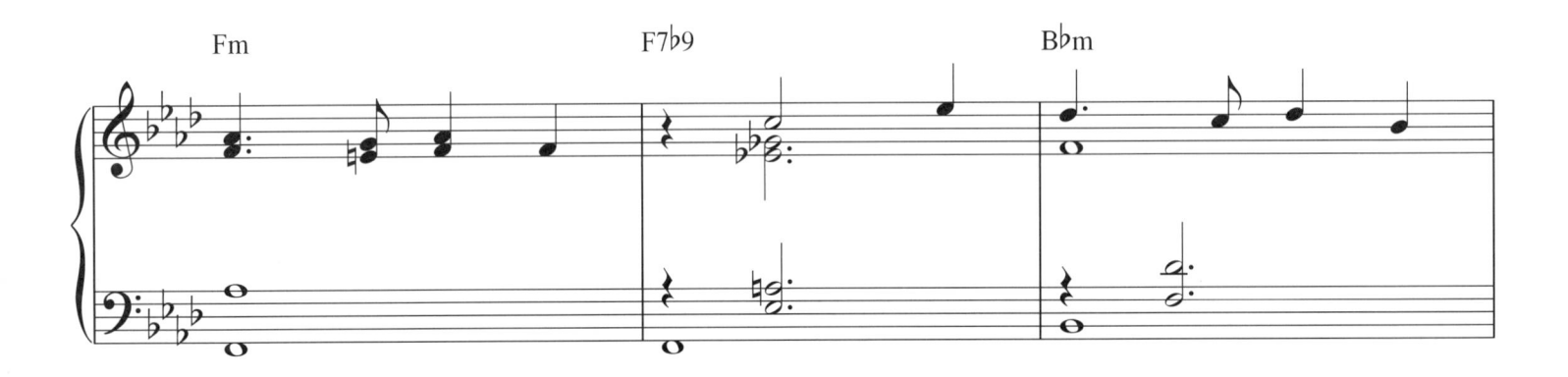

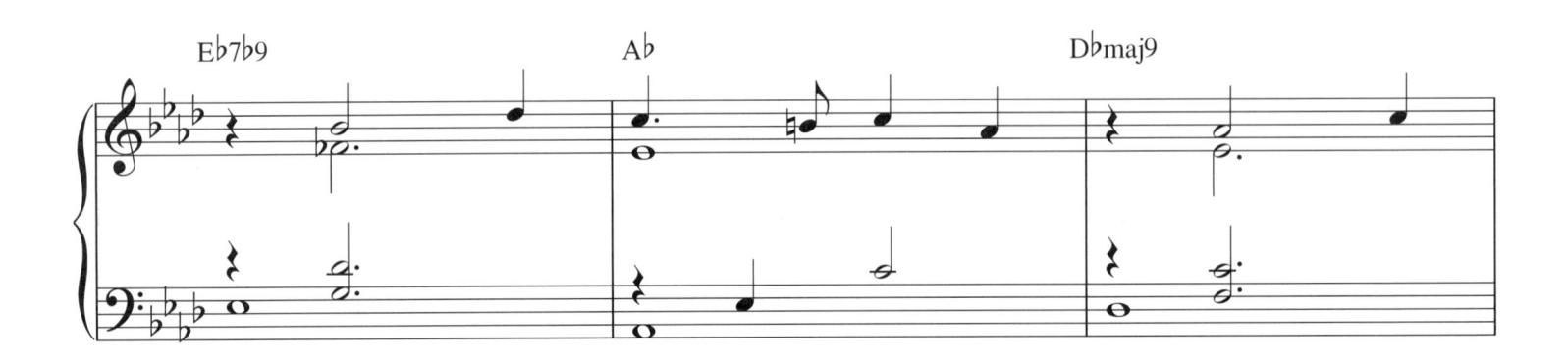

Fm(maj9) B♭m11 C7♯5 C7
B♭dim7/F Fm Fm(maj9) B♭m11
To Coda
C7♯5 C7 B♭dim7/F Fm
rit.
pp
Medium Swing
Fm Dm7♭5
mf
G7 C7 F7♭9 B♭m E♭7♭9 A♭
D♭7♯11 G7♭9 C7 Fm Dm7♭5

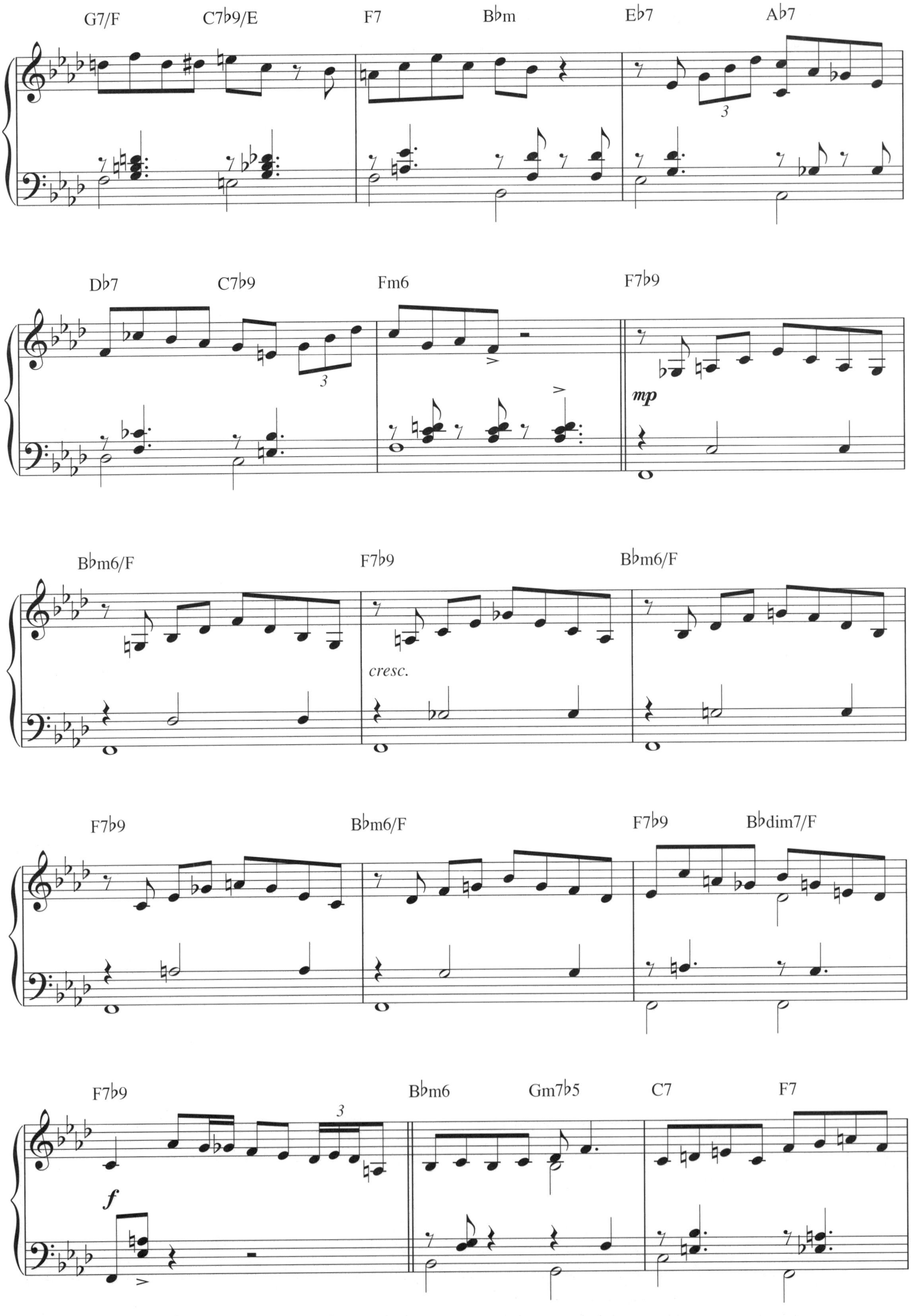
G7/F C7b9/E F7 Bbm Eb7 Ab7
Db7 C7b9 Fm6 F7b9
mp
Bbm6/F F7b9 Bbm6/F
cresc.
F7b9 Bbm6/F F7b9 Bbdim7/F
F7b9 Bbm6 Gm7b5 C7 F7
f

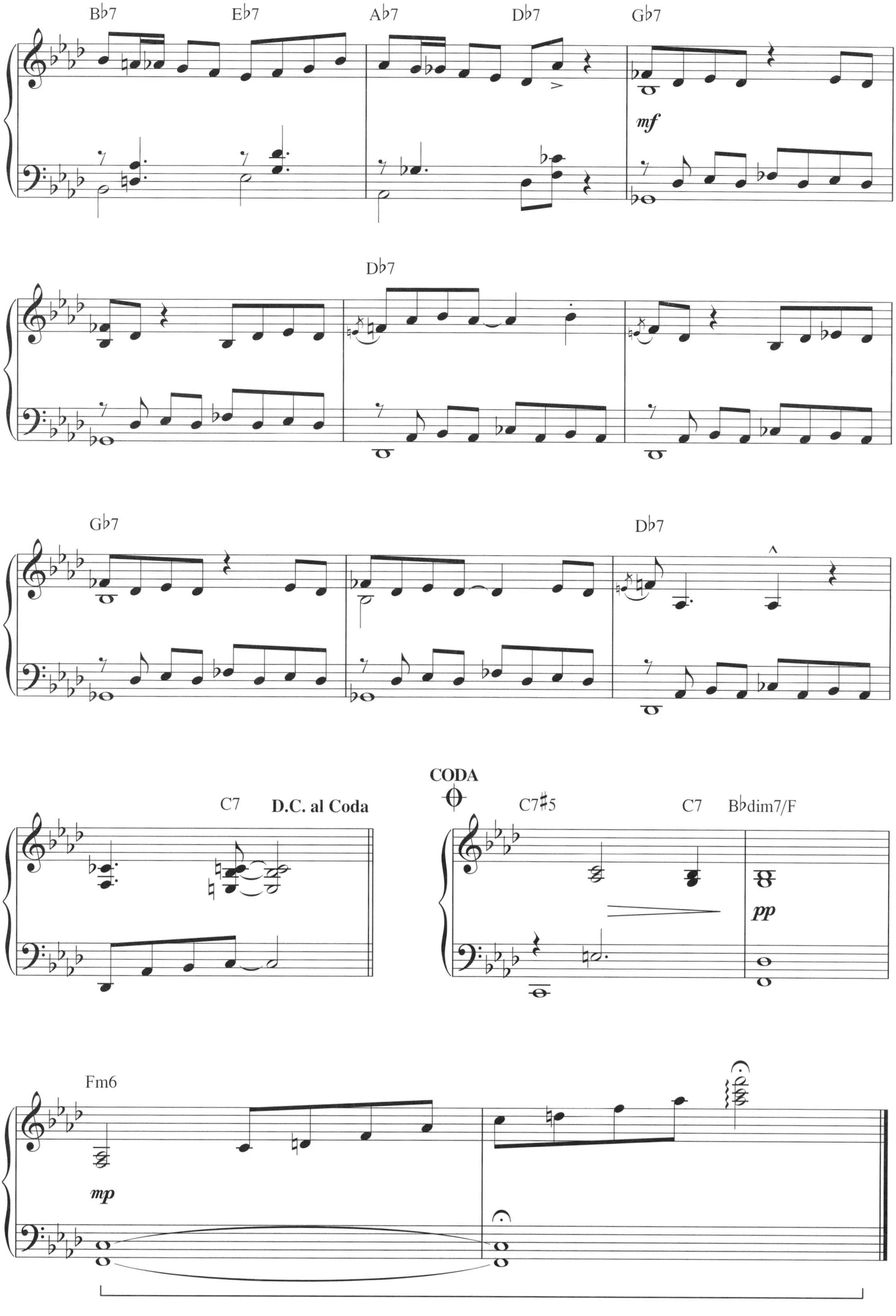
Bb7
Eb7
Ab7
Db7
Gb7
mf
Db7
Gb7
Db7
C7
D.C. al Coda
CODA
C7#5
C7
Bbdim7/F
pp
Fm6
mp

EMBRACEABLE YOU
from CRAZY FOR YOU

Music and Lyrics by GEORGE GERSHWIN
and IRA GERSHWIN

Whimsically

Dozens of girls would storm up; I had to lock my door. Somehow I couldn't warm up to one before. What was it that controlled me?

© 1930 (Renewed) WB MUSIC CORP.
All Rights Reserved Used by Permission

What kept my love-life lean? My in-tu-i-tion told me You'd come on the scene. La-dy, lis-ten to the rhy-thm of my heart-beat, And you'll get just what I mean.

Em-brace me, My sweet em-brace-a-ble you!

Am F7/A D7 G/B D7sus/A G
3fr
Em - brace me, You ir - re - place - a - ble you!
Em Em7/D Em6/C♯ F♯7 Bm Bm(maj7) Bm7 E9
7fr
Just one look at you, my heart grew tip - sy in me;
D/A D♯dim A9 D7
6fr
5fr
You and you a - lone bring out the gyp - sy in me!
G G♯dim7 D7/F♯ C(add2)/E Fm6 D7/F♯
I love all the man - y charms a - bout you;

Lyrics:

A-bove all, I want my arms a-bout you.

Don't be a naugh-ty ba-by, Come to pa-pa, Come to pa-pa, do! My sweet em-brace-a-ble you!

you!

ESTATE

Music by BRUNO MARTINO
Lyrics by BRUNO BRIGHETTI

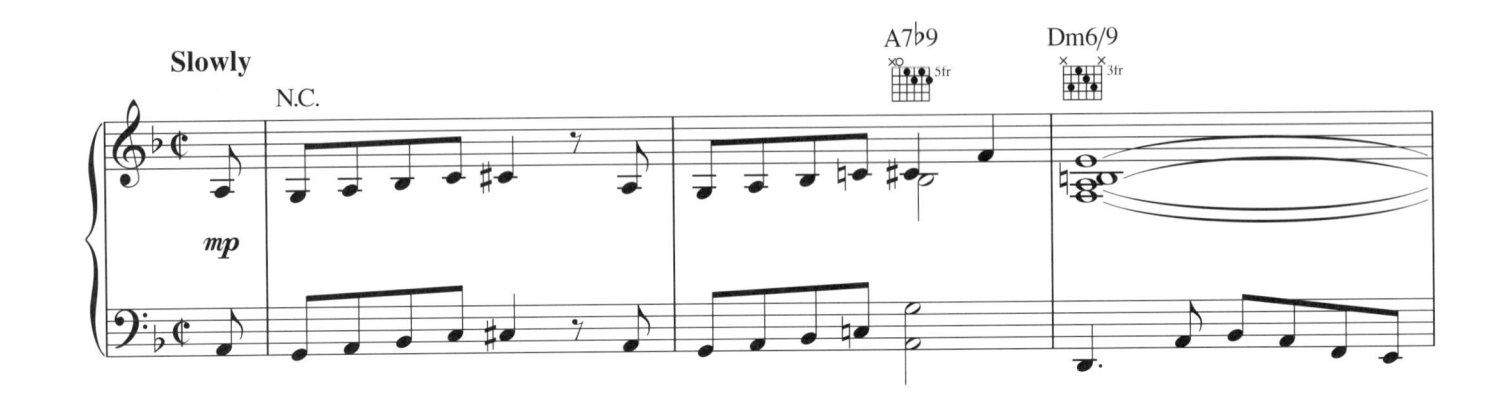

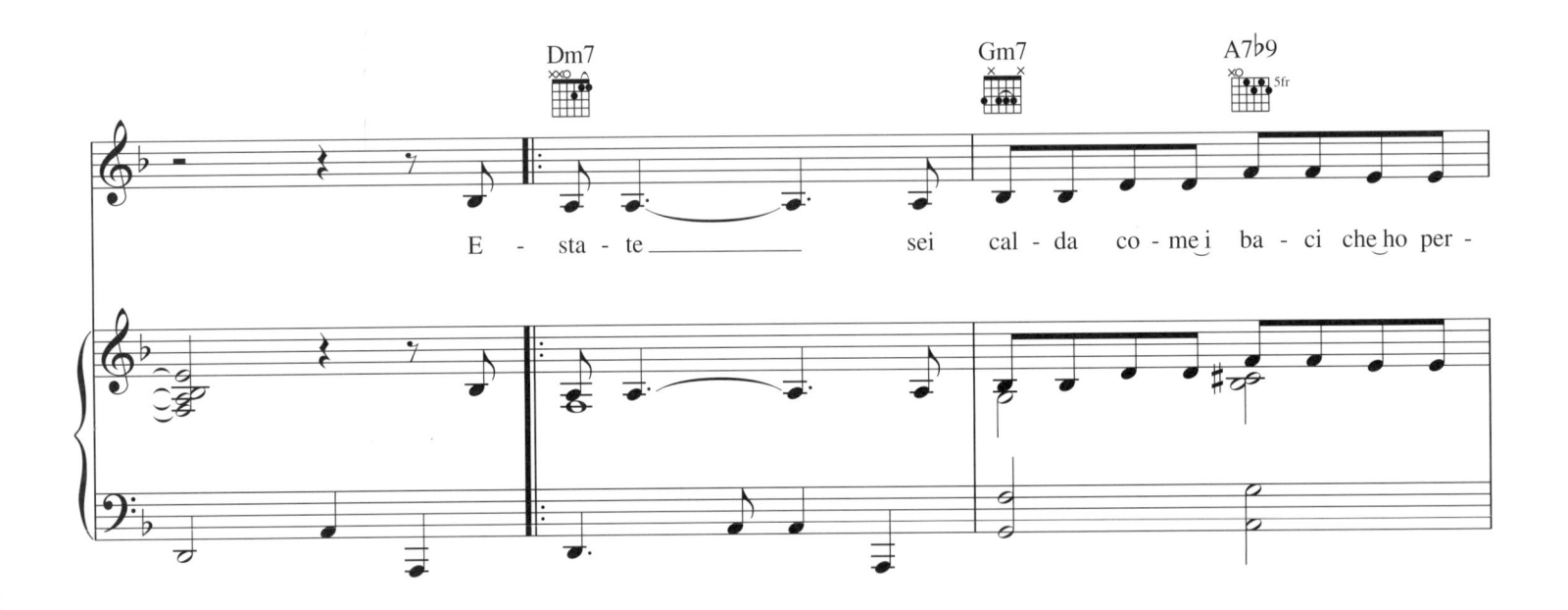

E - sta - te_____ sei cal - da co - me i ba - ci che ho per - du - to_____ sei pie - na di un a - mo - re che è pas - sa - to_____ che il

Copyright © 1960 SANTA CECILIA CASA MUSICALE
Copyright Renewed
All Rights for United States and Canada Controlled and Administered by UNIVERSAL MUSIC CORP.
All Rights Reserved Used by Permission

cuo - re mio vor - reb - be can - cel - lar. _____ O - dio l'e -

sta - te! _____ Il so - le che o - gni gior - no ci scal - da - va, _____ che

splen - di - di tra - mon - ti di - pin - ge - va _____ a -

des - so bru - cia so - lo con fu - ror. _____ Tor - ne - rá un al - tro in -

verno, — cadranno mille petali di rose — la neve coprirà tutte le cose — e forse un po' di pace tornerà! — Odio l'estate! che ha dato il suo profumo ad ogni fio - re, ___ l'e - sta - te che ha crea - to il no - stro a - mo - re ___ per far - mi poi mo - ri - re di do - lor! ___ O - dio l'e - sta - te! ___ O - dio l'e - sta - te! ___ E - sta - te! ___

Ev'ry Time We Say Goodbye

from SEVEN LIVELY ARTS

Words and Music by
COLE PORTER

E♭ Cm E♭ Cm E♭ Cm Fm7 B♭7
Ev - 'ry time we say good - bye I die a lit - tle,
E♭ B♭7 G♭ B♭7 E♭ E♭7
ev - 'ry time we say good - bye I won - der
A♭m E♭/G G♭dim7 Fm7♭5 B♭7
why a lit - tle, why the gods a - bove me who
B♭m/E♭ E♭7 A♭ Fm7♭5
must be in the know think so lit - tle

of me they al-low you to go. When you're near there's such an air of spring a-bout it, I can hear a lark some-where be-gin to sing a-bout it. There's no love song fin - er, but how strange the change from ma - jor to mi - nor

ev - 'ry time _____ we say good - bye. _____

_____ we say good - bye. Ev - 'ry sin - gle time we

say good - bye. _____

FASCINATING RHYTHM
from RHAPSODY IN BLUE

Music and Lyrics by GEORGE GERSHWIN
and IRA GERSHWIN

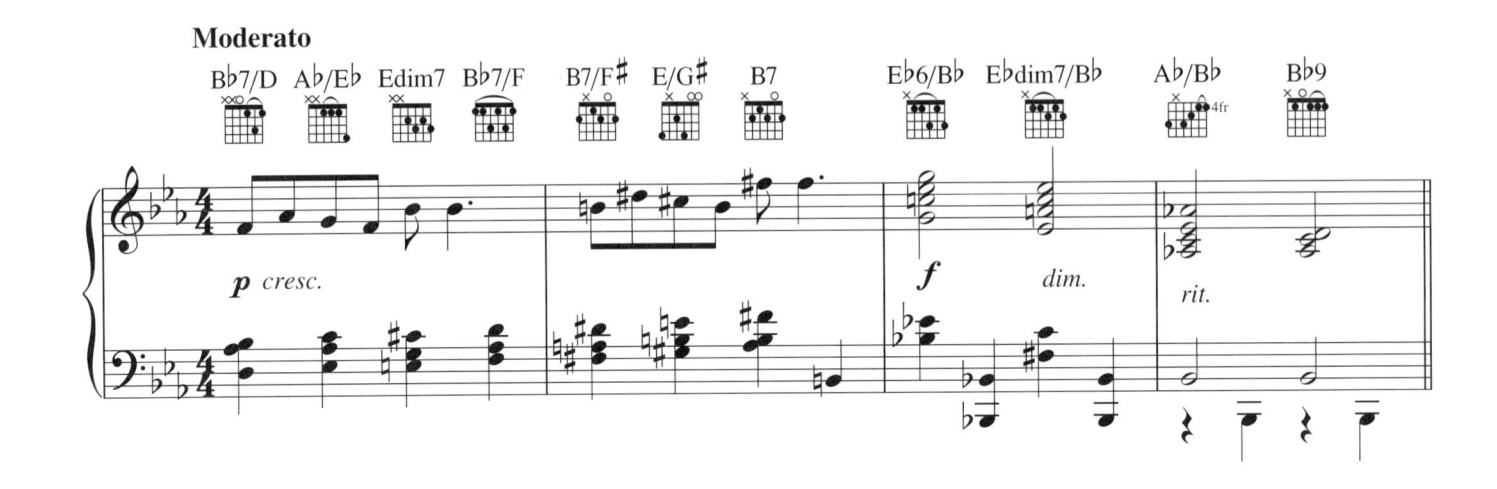

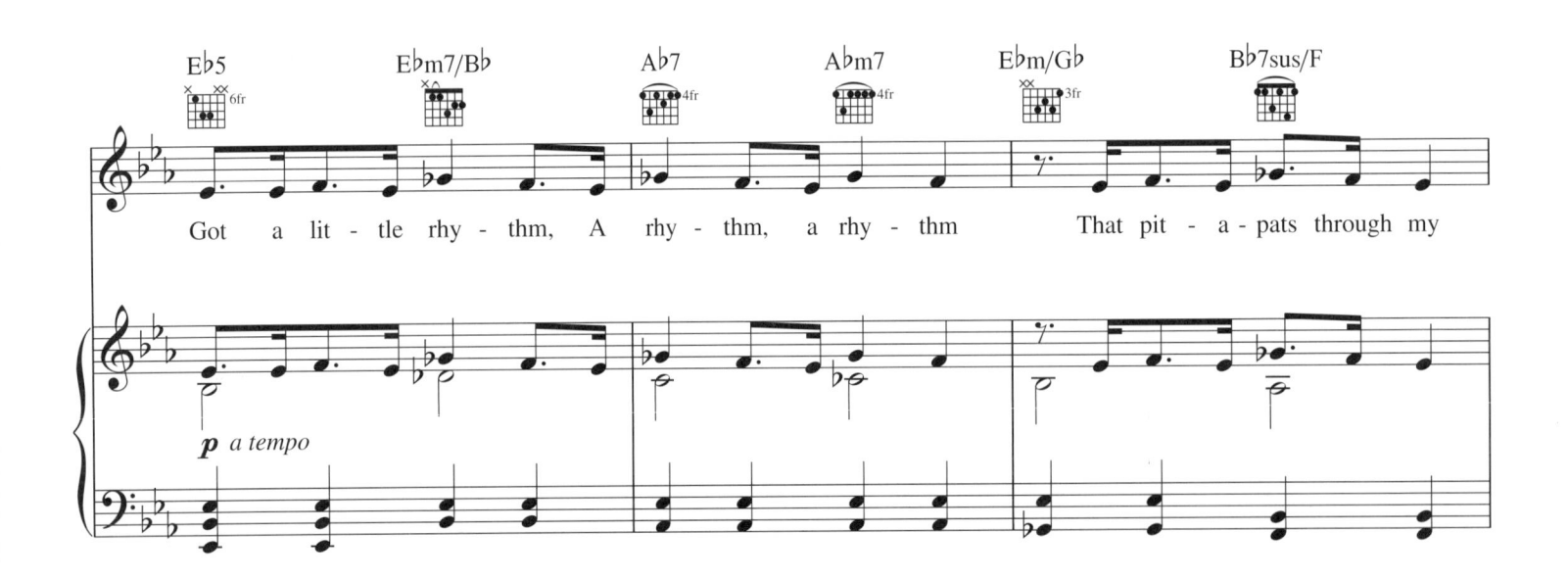

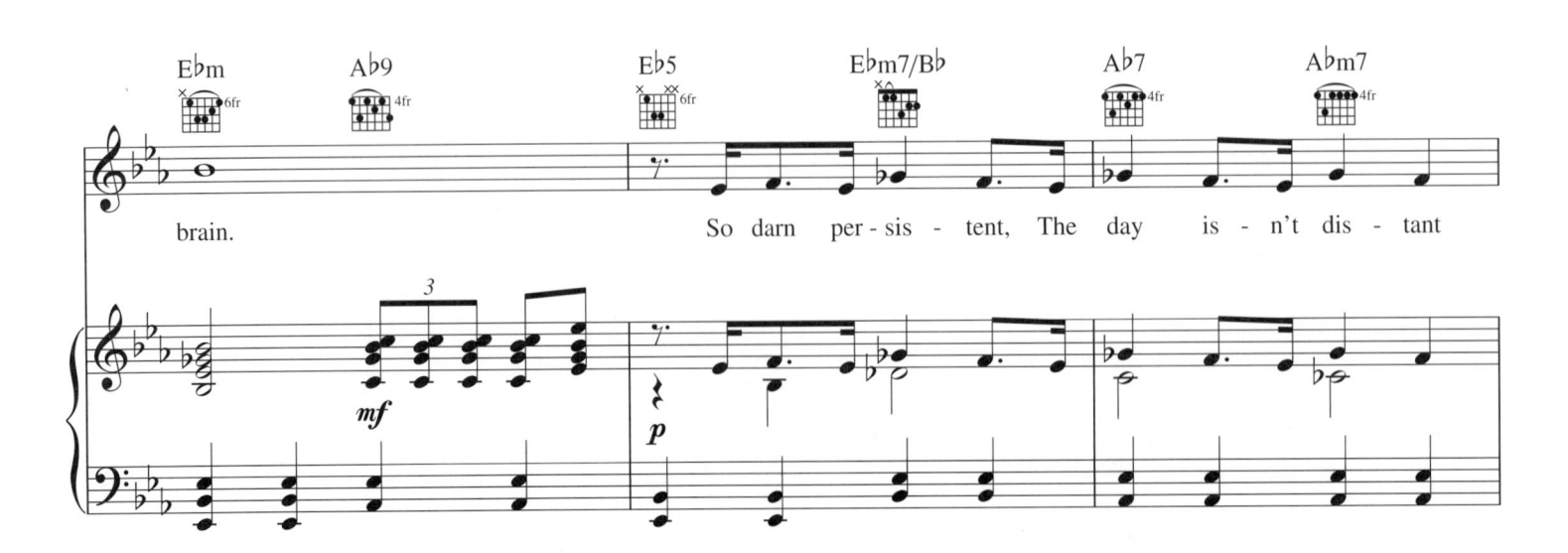

When it-'ll drive me in-sane. Comes in the morn-ing With-out an-y warn-ing, And hangs a-round all day. I'll have to sneak up to it, Some-day, and speak up to it, I hope it lis-tens when I say: "Fas-ci-nat-ing Rhy-thm You've got me on the go! Fas-ci-nat-ing Rhy-thm I'm all a-quiv-er. What a mess you're mak-ing! The

neigh-bors want to know why I'm al-ways shak-ing Just like a

fliv-er. Each morn-ing I get up with the

sun, (Start a-hop-ping, nev-er stop-ping) To find at

night, no work __ has been done. I know that once it didn't matter But now you're doing wrong; When you start to pat-ter, I'm so un-hap-py. Won't you take a day off? De-cide to run a-long Some-where far a-way off, And make it

126

FLY ME TO THE MOON
(In Other Words)

Words and Music by
BART HOWARD

hold my hand! In other words, darling, kiss me! Fill my heart with song, and let me sing for-ev-er-more; You are all I long for, all I wor-ship and a-dore. In

1
Fm7
A♭/B♭
D7♭9
Gm7♭5
C9
Cmaj7
oth - er words,
please be
true!
In
Fm7
A♭/B♭
B♭9
E♭(add9)
D♭
G7
oth - er words,
I love
you.
2
Gm7♭5
C9
C7♯5(♯9)
Fm7
A♭/B♭
true!
In
oth - er words,
B♭9
B♭7♭9
E♭6
N.C.
I love
you!
8vb

A FOGGY DAY
(In London Town)
from A DAMSEL IN DISTRESS

Music and Lyrics by GEORGE GERSHWIN
and IRA GERSHWIN

Moderately

mf

I was a stranger in the city. Out of town were the people I knew. I had that feeling of self-pity, What to do? What to do? What to do? The outlook was decidedly

© 1937 (Renewed) GEORGE GERSHWIN MUSIC and IRA GERSHWIN MUSIC
All Rights Administered by WB MUSIC CORP.
All Rights Reserved   Used by Permission

blue.____ But as I walked through the fog-gy streets a-lone, It turned out to be the luck-iest day I've known.____ A fog-gy day ____ in Lon-don town ____ Had me low ____ and had me down. ____

I viewed the morning with a-larm,_ The British Mu-se-um had lost its charm._ How long, I won-dered, could this thing last?_ But the age of mir-a-cles had-n't passed,_ For, sud - den - ly, _____ I saw you there _____ And through foggy London town the sun was shin - ing ev - 'ry - where. A where. _____

Gee Baby, Ain't I Good to You

Words by DON REDMAN and ANDY RAZAF
Music by DON REDMAN

Slow Blues

Love makes me treat you the way that I do.

Gee, ba-by, ain't I good to you! There's noth-in' too good for a

© 1929 CAPITOL SONGS, INC. and MICHAEL H. GOLDSEN, INC.
© Renewed 1957, 1985 MICHAEL H. GOLDSEN, INC. and EDWIN H. MORRIS & COMPANY, A Division of MPL Music Publishing, Inc.
All Rights Reserved

girl _____ that's so true. Gee, ba-by, ain't I good _____ to you! Bought you a fur coat for Christ-mas, a dia-mond ring, _____ a Cad-il-lac car an' ev-'ry-thing. _____ Love _____ makes me treat you the

To Coda
G7 C9 C7♭9 F7 F7♭5 B♭9 B♭7♭9
way that I do. Gee, baby, ain't I good to
1
E♭ F7 A♭7 G7
you!
2
E♭ Fm7 Fm7♭5 B♭7
you!
E♭6 Fm7 B♭7 E♭6 A♭6 B♭9
Lis - ten, lis - ten to what I have to say, what I want to tell
E♭6 B♭6/9 E♭6 Fm7 B♭7
you. Lis - ten, lis - ten to why I feel this way,
3fr
4fr

E♭6 A♭6 B♭9 E♭6 G7 G7♭5
just why I feel this way. Say, do you ev - er
C6/9 F7 F7♭5 B♭9
won - der just why I'm nev - er blue?
E♭7 E♭7♭5 A♭13 D♭9 Dm7♭5
Say do you ev - er won - der just why I'm so good to
G7
you?
D.S. al Coda
CODA
E♭ A♭m6 E♭maj7
you!

GIANT STEPS

By JOHN COLTRANE

Solo based on one by John Coltrane

G
C♯m9
F♯13
B6/9
Fm7
B♭7
E♭6/9
C♯m9
F♯13
3
B
D7
G
B♭7
E♭6/9
Am7
D7♯5(♯9)
G
B♭9
E♭
F♯13
Bmaj7
Fm9
B♭7
E♭6/9

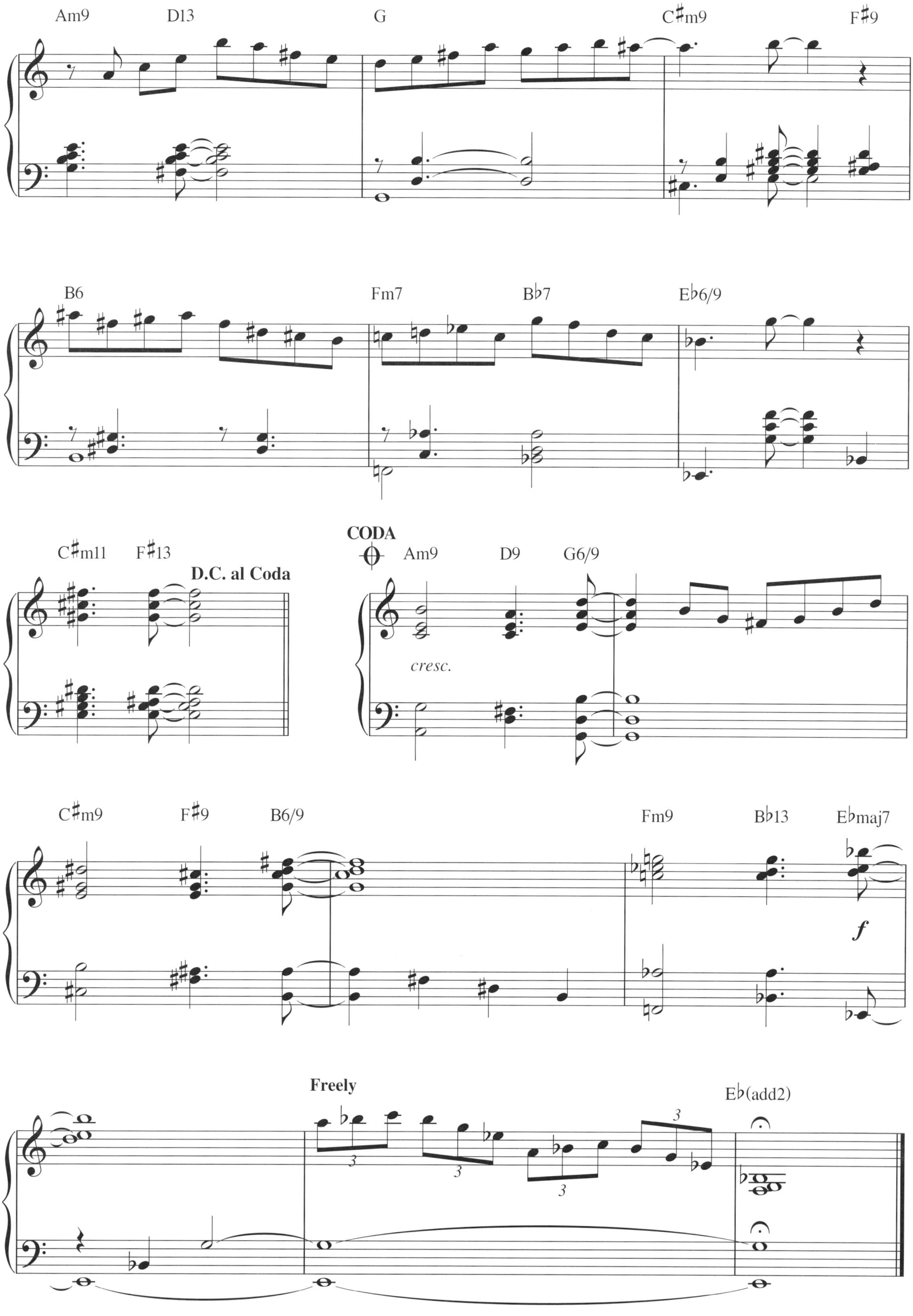
Am9
D13
G
C♯m9
F♯9
B6
Fm7
B♭7
E♭6/9
C♯m11
F♯13
D.C. al Coda
CODA
Am9
D9
G6/9
cresc.
C♯m9
F♯9
B6/9
Fm9
B♭13
E♭maj7
f
Freely
E♭(add2)

GIRL TALK

from the Paramount Picture HARLOW

Words by BOBBY TROUP
Music by NEAL HEFTI

be-comes es-sen-tial things that wom-en find so "ap-pro-po." But that's a dame, {they're/we're} all the same,

it's just a game. {They/We} call it Girl Talk, Girl Talk.

{They/We} all me-ow a-bout the ups and downs of all {their/our} friends,

the "who," the "how," the "why," {they/we} dish the dirt, it nev-er ends. The weak-er sex, the speak-er sex {we/you} mortal males behold; but tho' we joke, we wouldn't trade you for a ton of gold.

So, baby, stay and gab away, but hear me say that after
(It's all been planned, so take my hand, please understand the sweetest

Girl Talk, talk to me.
Girl Talk talks of you.)

me.
you.)

HOW DEEP IS THE OCEAN
(How High Is the Sky)

Words and Music by
IRVING BERLIN

Moderately

How much do I love you? I'll tell you no lie, how deep is the o-cean, how high is the sky? How man-y

© Copyright 1932 by Irving Berlin
Copyright Renewed
International Copyright Secured   All Rights Reserved

times a day ___ do I think of you? ___

How man-y ros - es are sprin-kled with dew? ___

How far would I trav-el

to be where you are? How far is the

jour - ney from here to a star? And if I ev - er lost you, how much would I cry? How deep is the o - cean, how high is the sky? sky?

HOW ABOUT YOU?

Words by RALPH FREED
Music by BURTON LANE

will de - pend on lit - tle plea - sures they will share.

So let us com - pare.

Moderately, with expression

I like New York in June, how a - bout you? ___

___ I like a Gersh - win tune,

how a-bout you? _____ I love a fire-side when a storm is due. _____ I like po-ta-to chips, moon-light and mo-tor trips, how a-bout you? _____ I'm mad a-bout good books, can't get my fill.

And Franklin Roosevelt's looks, give me a thrill. Holding hands in a movie show, when all the lights are low may not be new. But I like it, how about you? you?

HOW LONG HAS THIS BEEN GOING ON?
from ROSALIE

Music and Lyrics by GEORGE GERSHWIN
and IRA GERSHWIN

Moderately

Bill: As a tot, when I trot-ted in lit-tle vel-vet pant - ies,
Mary: 'Neath the stars, at ba-zaars, of-ten I've had to ca-ress men.

I was kissed by my sis-ters, my cous-ins and my aunt - ies.
Five or ten dol-lars, then, I'd col-lect from all those yes - men.

Sad to tell, it was Hell, an in-fer-no worse than Dan - te's.
Don't be sad; I must add that they meant no more than chess - men.

© 1927 (Renewed) WB MUSIC CORP.
All Rights Reserved   Used by Permission

A7 Em7/A A7 Am D7
So, my dear, I swore, "Nev - er, nev - er - more!"
Dar - ling, can't you see 'twas for char - i - ty?
G Em7 Am7 D7 G G6 G
On my list, I in - sist - ed that kiss - ing must be crossed out.
Though these lips have made slips, it was nev - er real - ly se - rious.
G♯m7♭5 C♯7 F♯7♯5 F♯7♭9 Bm Bm/A G♯dim7
Now I find I was blind, and oh la - dy, how I've lost out!
Who'd a' thought I'd be brought to a state that's so de - li - rious?
molto rall.
Moderately slow
D13 Ddim7 D13 D9♯5 G9 C7 Cm7
I could cry salt - y tears; where have I been all these years?

G/B Bbdim7 Am7 D7 G7 C D7
Lit - tle wow, tell me now. How long has this been go - ing on?
Lis - ten, you, tell me, do. How long has this been go - ing on?
G D13 4fr Ddim7 D13 4fr D9#5 4fr G7
There were chills up my spine, and some thrills I
What a kick! How I buzz! Boy, you click as
C7 Cm7 3fr G/B Bbdim7 Am7 D7 G7
can't de - fine. Lis - ten, sweet, I re - peat: How
no one does! Hear me, sweet, I re - peat: How
C D7 G Cm/G 3fr Gdim7 G7 Cmaj7 F9 Cmaj7 F9
long has this been go - ing on? Oh, I feel that I could melt;
long has this been go - ing on? Dear, when in your arms I creep,

into Heav - en I'm hurled! _____ I know how Co - lum - bus felt _____
that di - vine ren - dez - vous, _____ don't wake me if I'm a - sleep, _____

find - ing an - oth - er world! Kiss me once, ___ then once more; ___
let me dream that it's true. Kiss me twice, ___ then once more; ___

what a dunce I was be - fore! ___ What a break! _____ For Heav - en's sake! _____ How
that makes thrice, let's make it four! ___ What a break! _____ For Heav - en's sake! _____ How

long has this been go - ing on? _____
long has this been go - ing on? ___

I GOT RHYTHM

from GIRL CRAZY
from AN AMERICAN IN PARIS

Music and Lyrics by GEORGE GERSHWIN
and IRA GERSHWIN

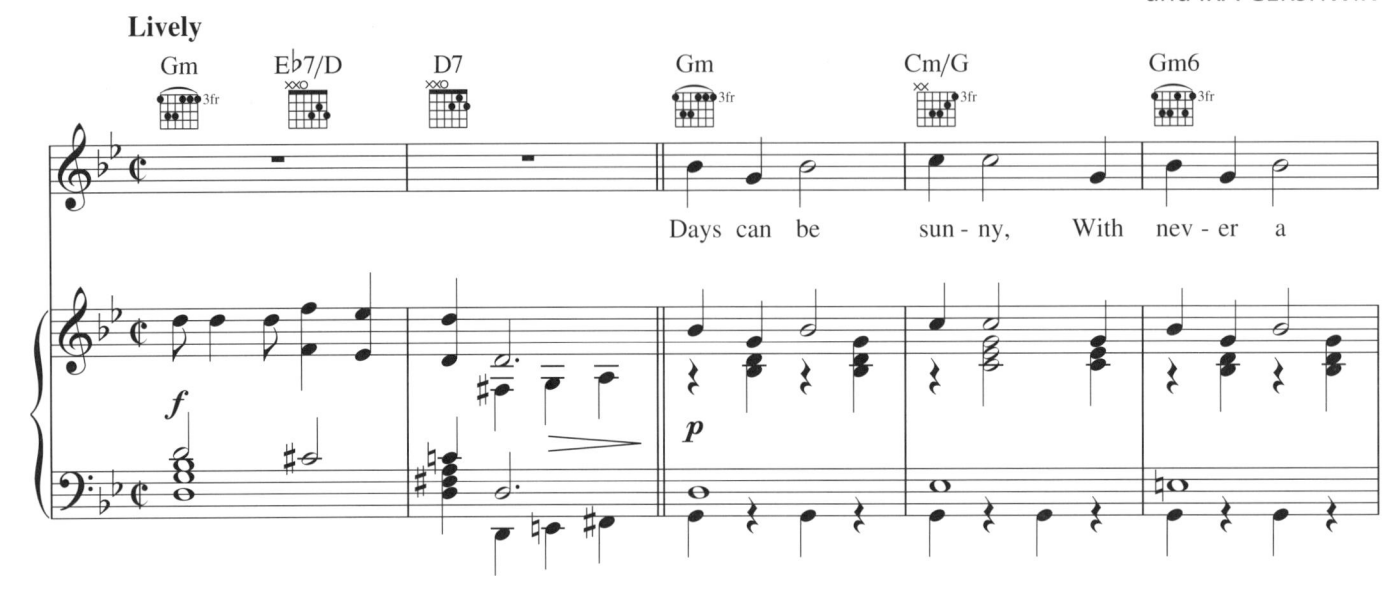

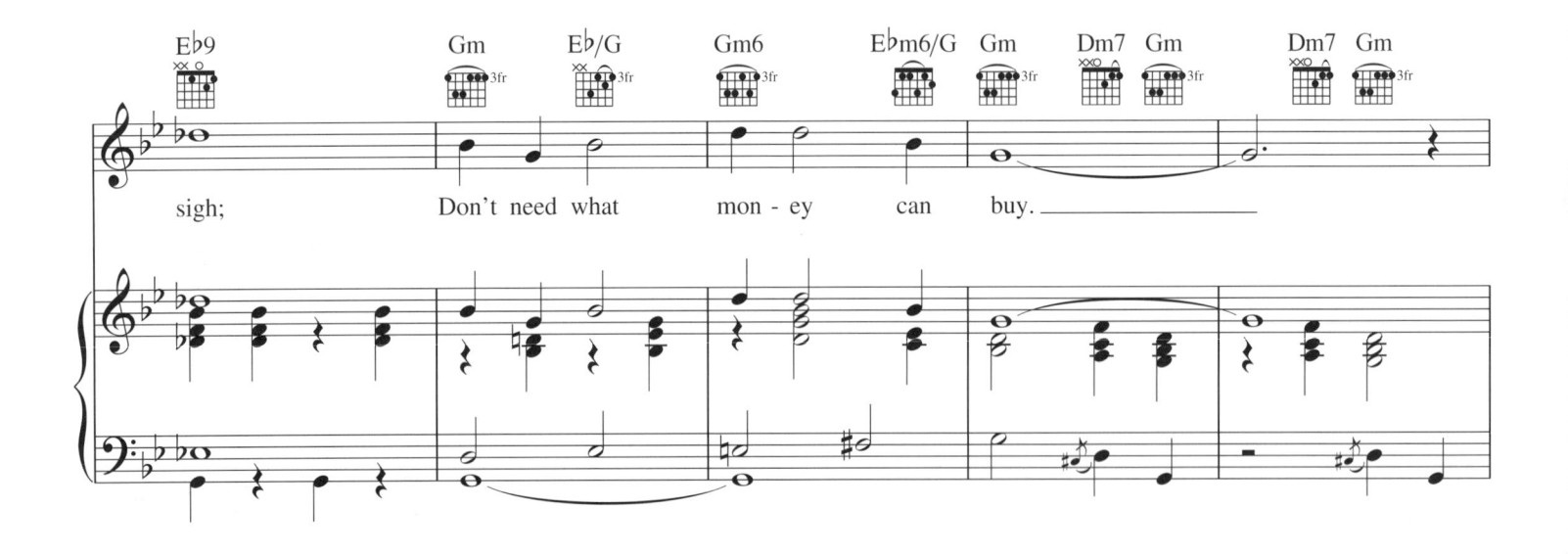

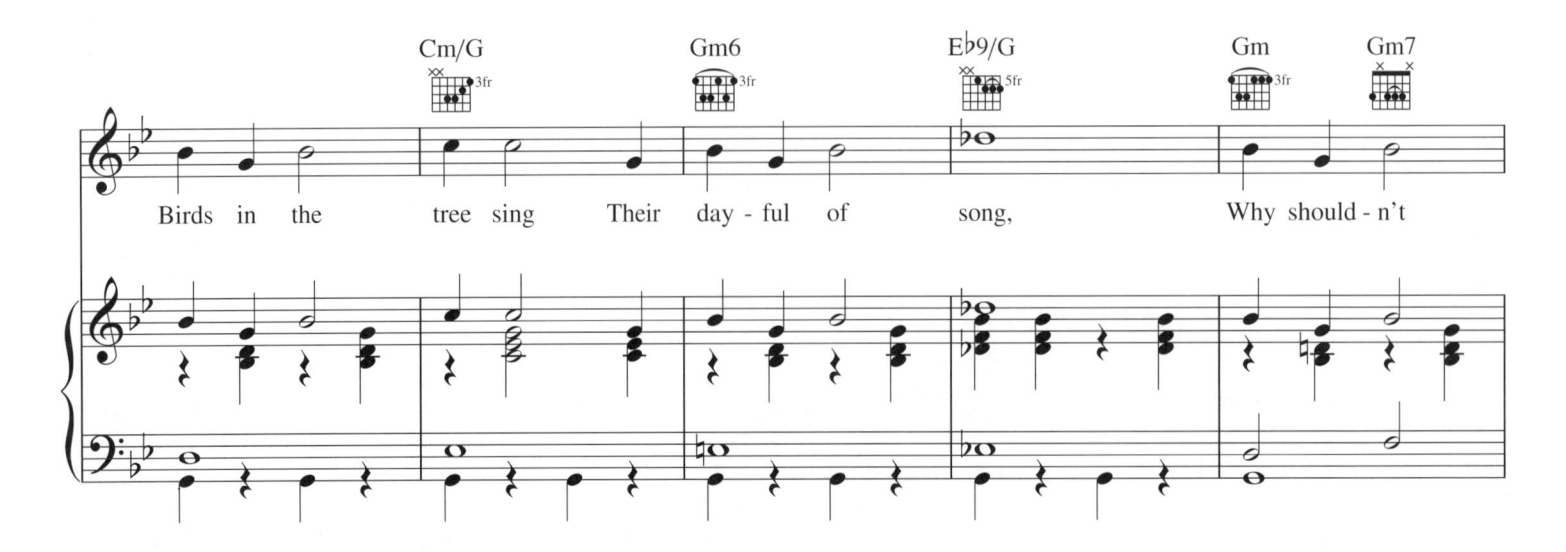

Lively

Days can be sun-ny, With nev-er a sigh; Don't need what mon-ey can buy.

Birds in the tree sing Their day-ful of song, Why should-n't

© 1930 (Renewed) WB MUSIC CORP.
All Rights Reserved   Used by Permission

we sing a-long? _____ I'm chip-per all the day, Hap-py with my lot. How do I get that way? Look at what I've got: I ___ got rhy-thm, __ I ___ got mu-sic, ___ I ___ got my man. __ Who could

ask for an-y-thing more? I got dais-ies

In green pas-tures, I got my man. Who could

ask for an-y-thing more? Old Man Trou-ble,

I don't mind him, You won't find him

G♭7♭5 F7 C7 F7 B♭ B♭6
'Round my door. I got
Cm7 F7 B♭6/F Edim/F Cm7 F7sus F7
star - light, I got sweet dreams,
B♭ B♭6 Cm7 F7 E♭m6/F B♭ A♭6
I got my man. Who could ask for an - y - thing
G7 C9 F7 B♭ A♭ G♭ D♭ B♭
more? Who could ask for an - y - thing more? more?
1
2
3fr
4fr

I'LL REMEMBER APRIL

Words and Music by PAT JOHNSTON,
DON RAYE and GENE DePAUL

Moderately, with expression

This love-ly day will length-en in-to eve-ning; we'll sigh good-bye to all we've ev-er had. A-lone, where we have walked to-geth-er, I'll re-

© 1941, 1942 (Renewed) PIC CORPORATION and UNIVERSAL MUSIC CORP.
All Rights Reserved

- member A - pril and be glad. I'll be con - tent you loved me once in A - pril. Your lips were warm and love and spring were new. But I'm not a - fraid of au - tumn and her sor-row, _____ for I'll re-mem-ber _____ A-pril and

you. _____ The fire will dwin-dle in-to

glow-ing ash-es, for flames and love live such a

lit-tle while. _____ I won't for-get, _____

but I won't be lonely. I'll remember April and I'll smile. smile.

IF I HAD YOU

Words and Music by TED SHAPIRO,
JIMMY CAMPBELL and REG CONNELLY

I dream'd all my dreams and schem'd all my schemes, but somehow it just seem'd wrong; Un to

My whole life would be just heaven to me, dear, if you'd learn to care, to

© 1928 (Renewed) CAMPBELL, CONNELLY & CO., LTD.
All Rights for the U.S. and Canada Administered by EMI ROBBINS CATALOG INC. (Publishing) and ALFRED MUSIC (Print)
All Rights Reserved Used by Permission

| Gm | A7 | D7 | G7 | C13 | C7(add13) |

til I met you ___ and then, dear, I knew ___ to me you must ___ be -
know all the bliss ___ of your lov-ing kiss ___ was wait-ing for me ___ some -

| F7 | Fdim7 | F7 | B♭ | | B♭7 |

long.
where. } I could show the world how to smile, I could be

| E♭6/B♭ | E♭maj7/B♭ | E♭m6 | B♭ | Edim7 |

glad all of the while, I could change the grey skies to

| F9 | F7♯5 | B♭/D | D♭dim7 | Cm7 | F6 | Gdim7 | Adim7 |

blue if I had you. ___

I could leave the old days be-hind, leave all my pals, I'd nev-er mind, I could start my life all a-new if I had you. I could climb the snow-capp'd moun-tains, sail the might-y o-cean wide, I could cross the burn-ing

167

IN YOUR OWN SWEET WAY

By DAVE BRUBECK

Medium Swing ($\sqrt{} = \sqrt{}^{3}\sqrt{}$)

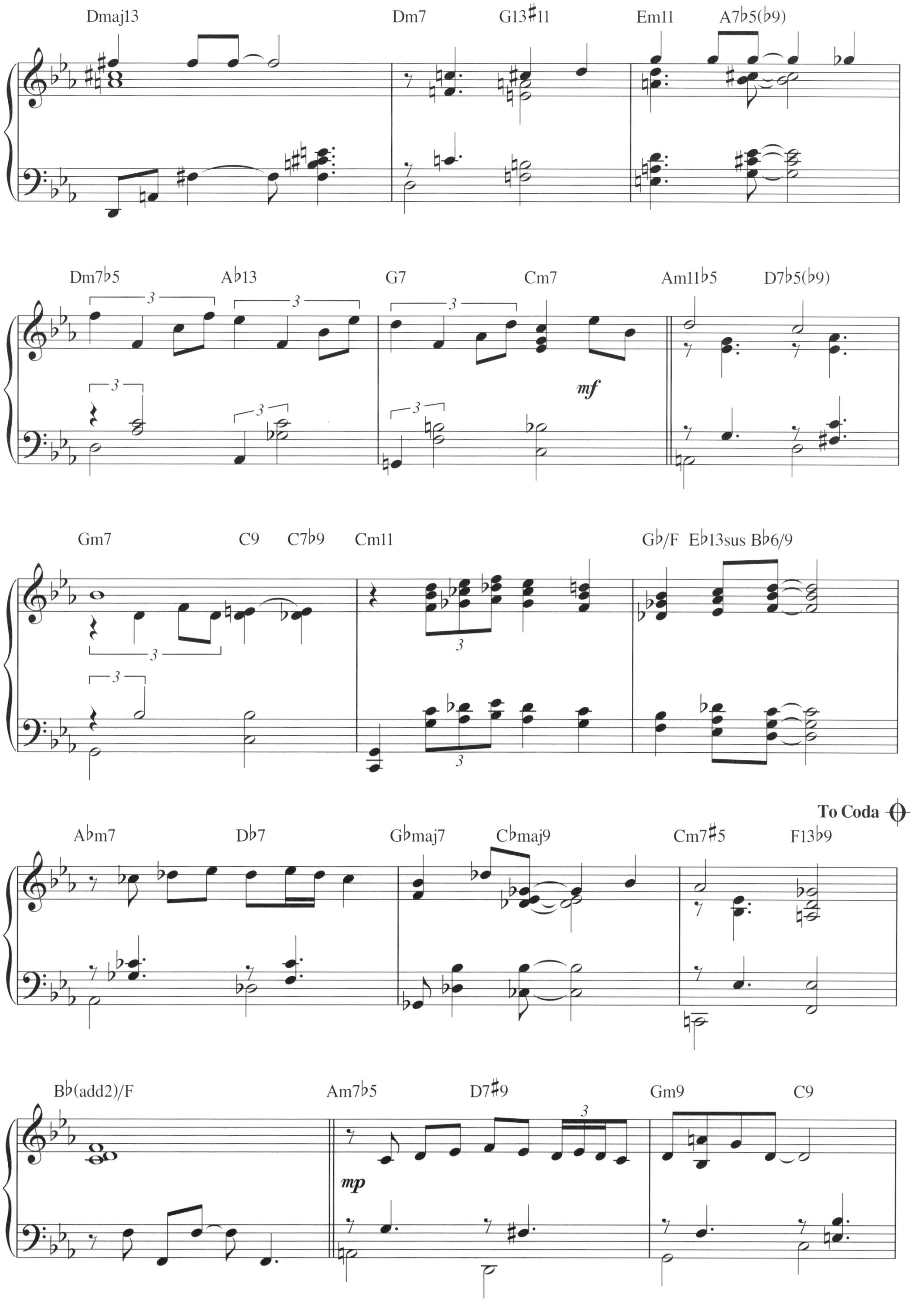
Dmaj13
Dm7
G13♯11
Em11
A7♭5(♭9)
Dm7♭5
A♭13
G7
Cm7
mf
Am11♭5
D7♭5(♭9)
Gm7
C9
C7♭9
Cm11
G♭/F
E♭13sus
B♭6/9
To Coda
A♭m7
D♭7
G♭maj7
C♭maj9
Cm7♯5
F13♭9
B♭(add2)/F
Am7♭5
D7♯9
mp
Gm9
C9

Cm7 F7♯9 3 B♭6/9 E♭maj13 A♭m7 D♭7
G♭maj7 Cm11 F7♯5(♯9) B♭6/9
Am11♭5 D7♯5(♯9) mf Gm9 3 Cm7 F7♯9
B♭maj7 A♭m7 D♭7 G♭maj7
Cm7 F7♯9 B♭maj7 Em11 A7♯5 D5 ff

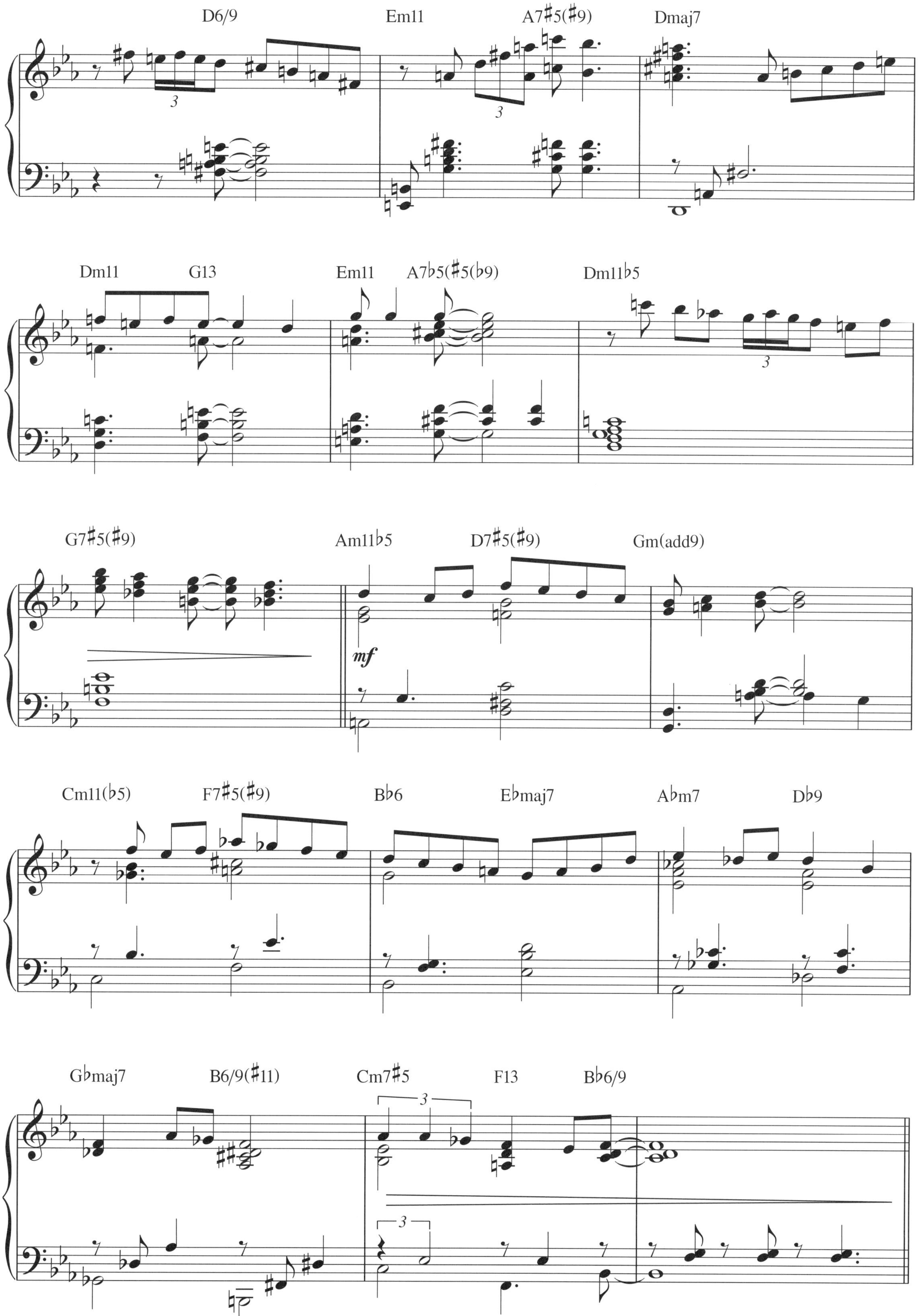
D6/9
Em11
A7♯5(♯9)
Dmaj7
3
3
Dm11
G13
Em11
A7♭5(♯5(♭9)
Dm11♭5
3
G7♯5(♯9)
Am11♭5
D7♯5(♯9)
Gm(add9)
mf
Cm11(♭5)
F7♯5(♯9)
B♭6
E♭maj7
A♭m7
D♭9
G♭maj7
B6/9(♯11)
Cm7♯5
F13
B♭6/9
3
3

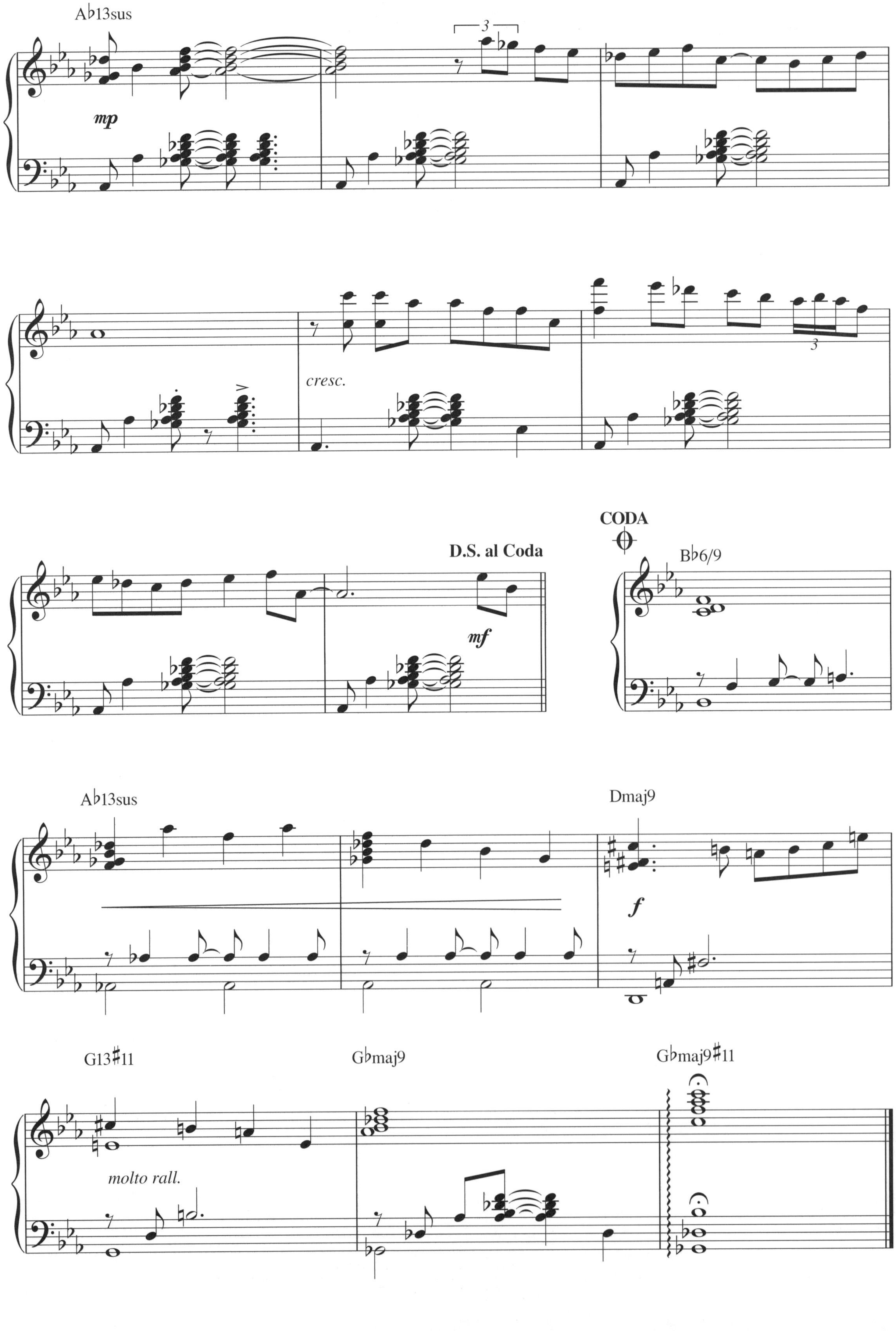
A♭13sus
mp
3
cresc.
3
D.S. al Coda
mf
CODA
B♭6/9
A♭13sus
Dmaj9
f
G13♯11
G♭maj9
G♭maj9♯11
molto rall.

LAURA

Lyric by JOHNNY MERCER
Music by DAVID RAKSIN

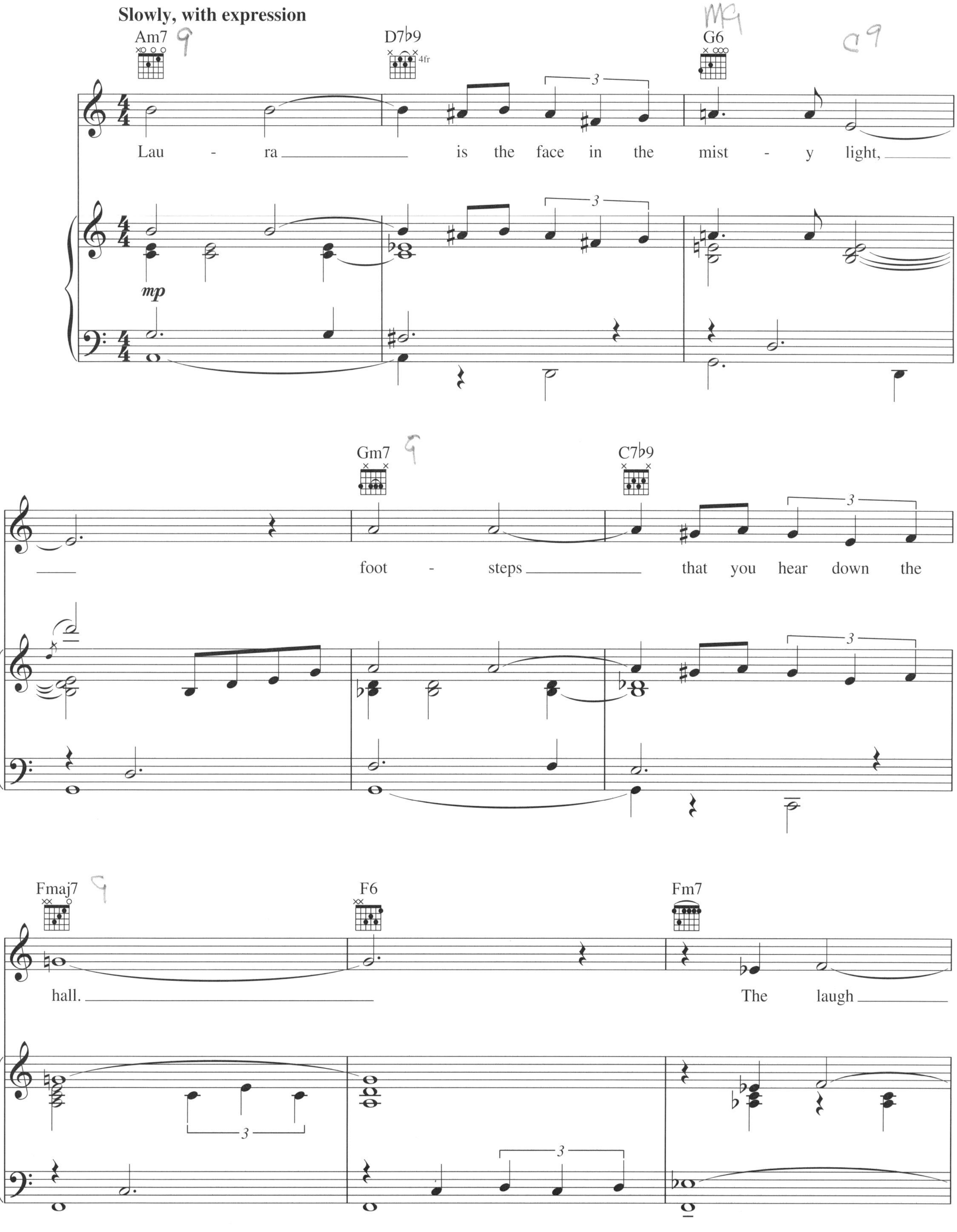

that floats on a sum - mer night that you can nev - er quite re - call. And you see Lau - ra on the train that is pass - ing thru, those eyes

175

IT HAD TO BE YOU

Words by GUS KAHN
Music by ISHAM JONES

Moderate Swing

Why do I do just as you say,
Seems like dreams like I al-ways had,
why must I just give you your way?
could be, should be mak-ing me glad.
Why do I sigh,
Why am I blue?

© 1924 (Renewed) GILBERT KEYES MUSIC and THE BANTAM MUSIC PUBLISHING CO.
All Rights Administered by WB MUSIC CORP.
All Rights Reserved Used by Permission

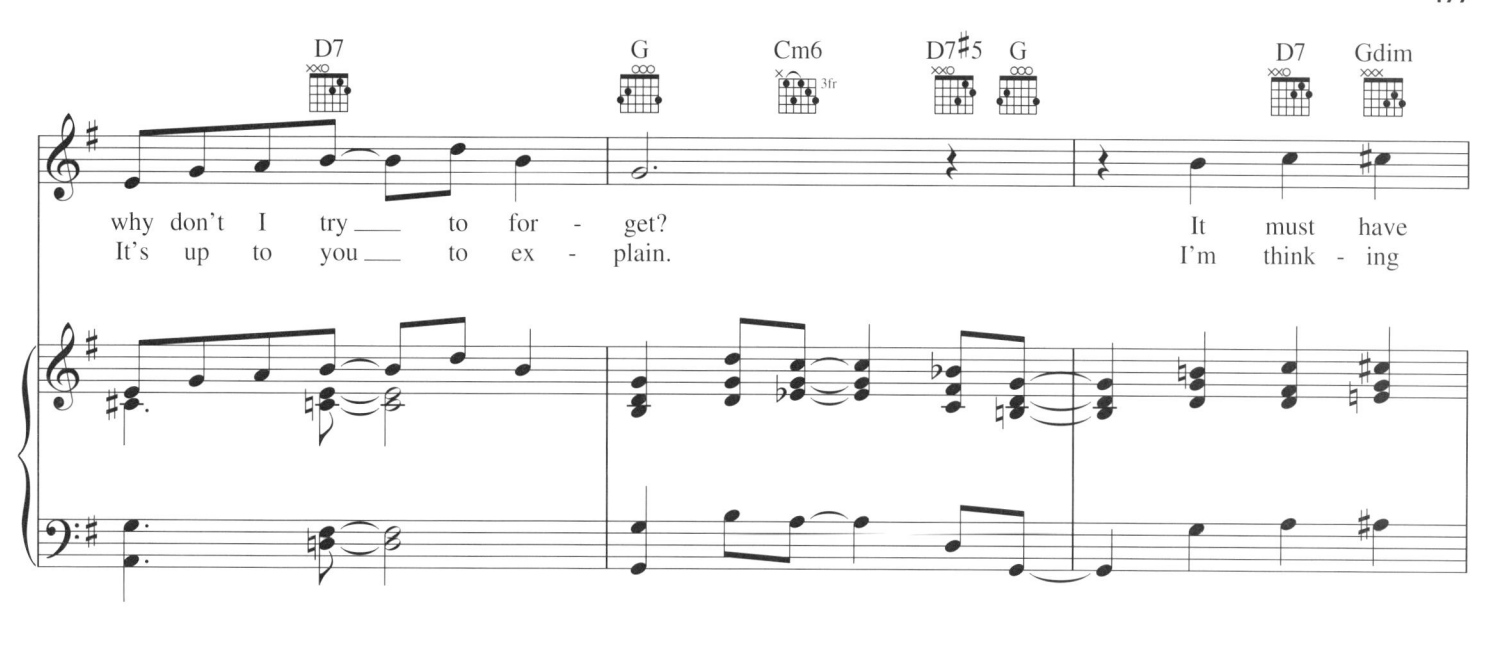

why don't I try to for - get? It must have
It's up to you to ex - plain. I'm think - ing

been that some - thing lov - ers call fate kept on say - ing
may - be, ba - by, I'll go a - way, some - day, some way,

I had to wait. I saw them all, just could - n't fall 'til we
you'll come and say: "It's you I need, and you'll be plead - ing in

met. / *vain.* It had to be you, it had to be you, I wandered around and finally found the somebody who

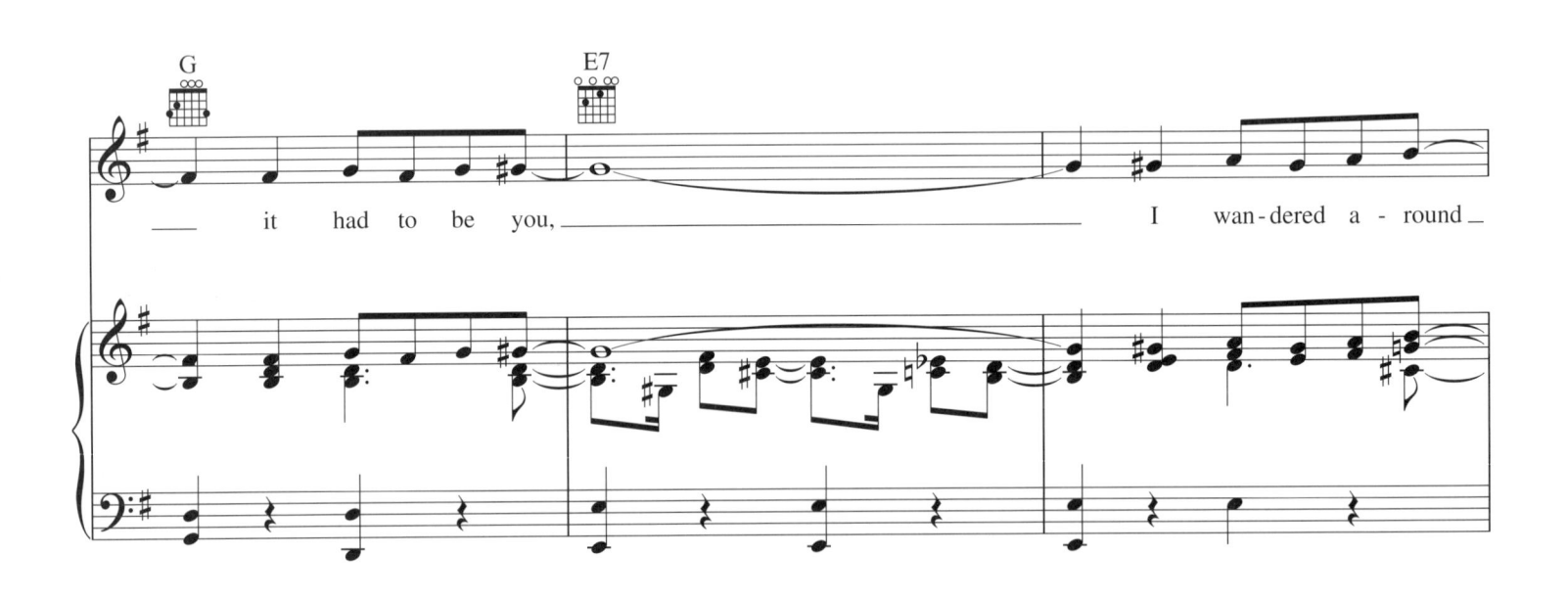

D7
D♯dim
could make me be true,
could make me be blue,
Em
A7
and e - ven be glad,
just to be sad,
D7
E♭7♭5
D7
D+
thinking - ing of you.
Some oth - ers I've seen

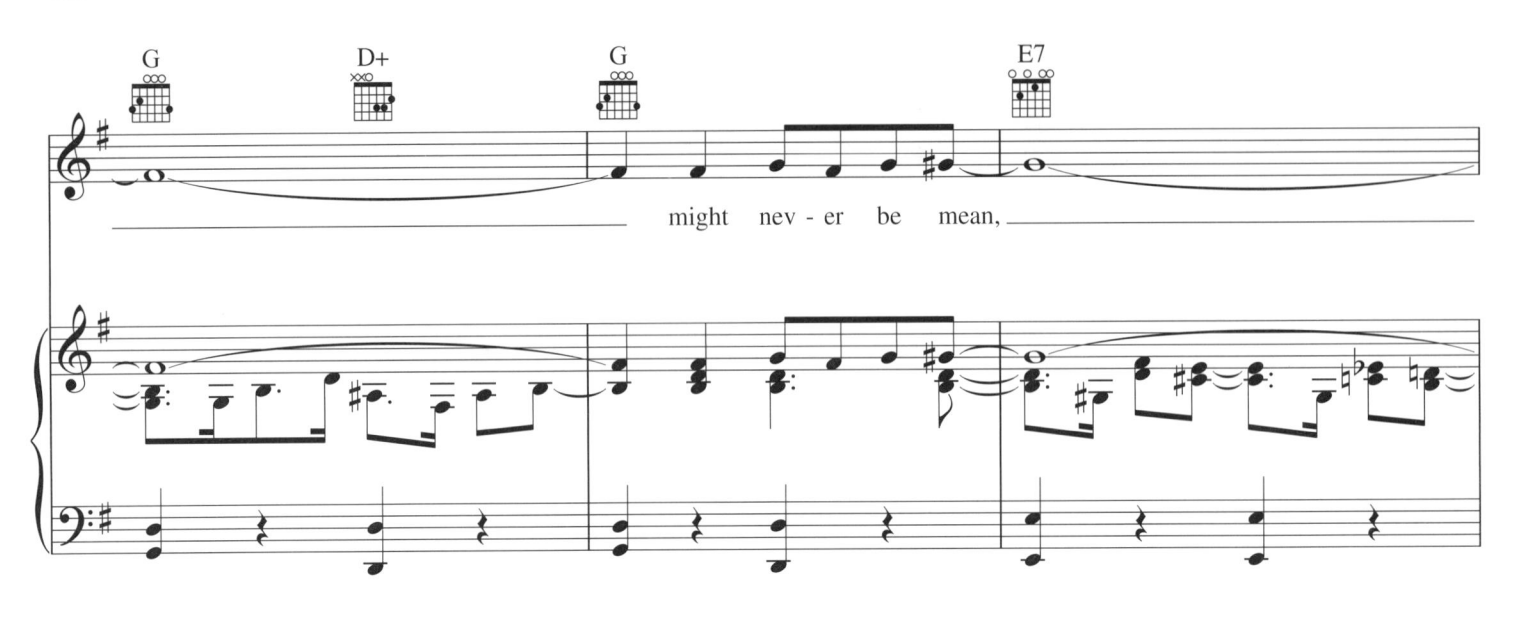

might nev-er be mean, might nev-er be cross or try to be boss, but they would-n't do. For no-bod-y else gave me a thrill,

181

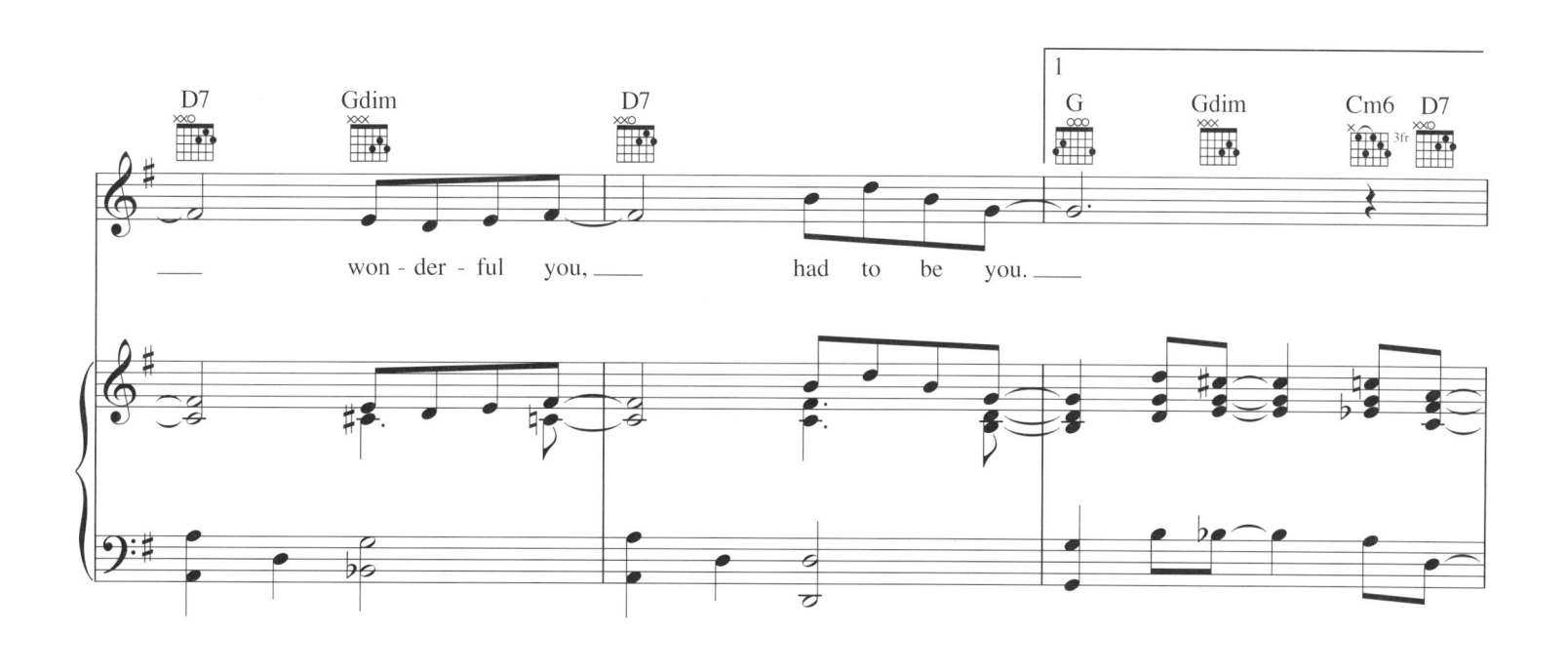

JUMPIN' AT THE WOODSIDE

Music by COUNT BASIE
Words by JON HENDRICKS

Bright Bounce

I gotta go. _____ I wanna blow. _____

I gotta go. _____

I got a
I never
A tiny

really groovy pad, a better pad I never had. I gotta
ever wanna move, I never had a better groove. I gotta
room is all I rent, but, man, I

really do a lot of livin'.

© 1935, 1959 (Copyrights Renewed) WB MUSIC CORP.
All Rights Reserved   Used by Permission

183

G6

Jump - in'! You dig it com - in' through the door, a lot a - jump - in'! And you can
jump - in'! You dig it soon as you ar - rive, a lot a - jump - in'! It's got an -

Am9 **Am9/D**

feel the shak - in' floor, a lot of jump - in'! And you'll be com - in' back for more. } I tell you
oth - er kind of jive, a lot of jump - in'! And real - ly ver - y much a - live.

G6   **1.** **D9** **G6**   **2.** **D9** **G6**

jump - in', man, they're jump - in' at the Wood - side now. A lot a Wood - side now!

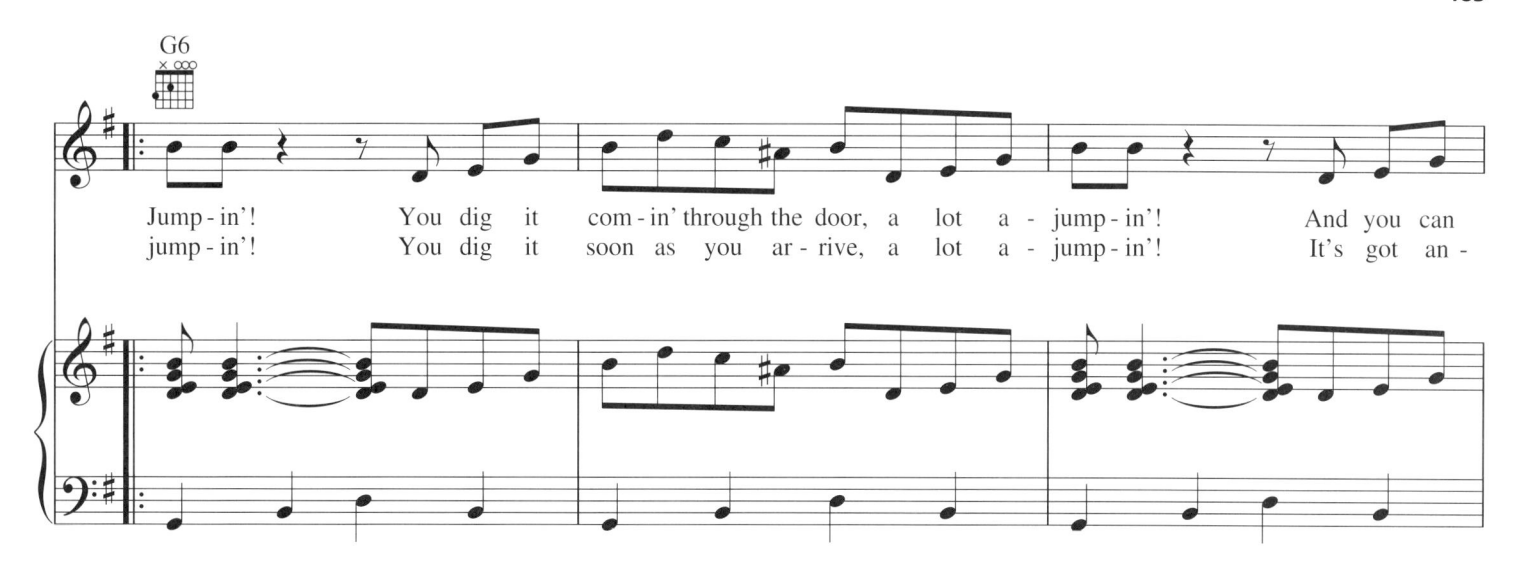

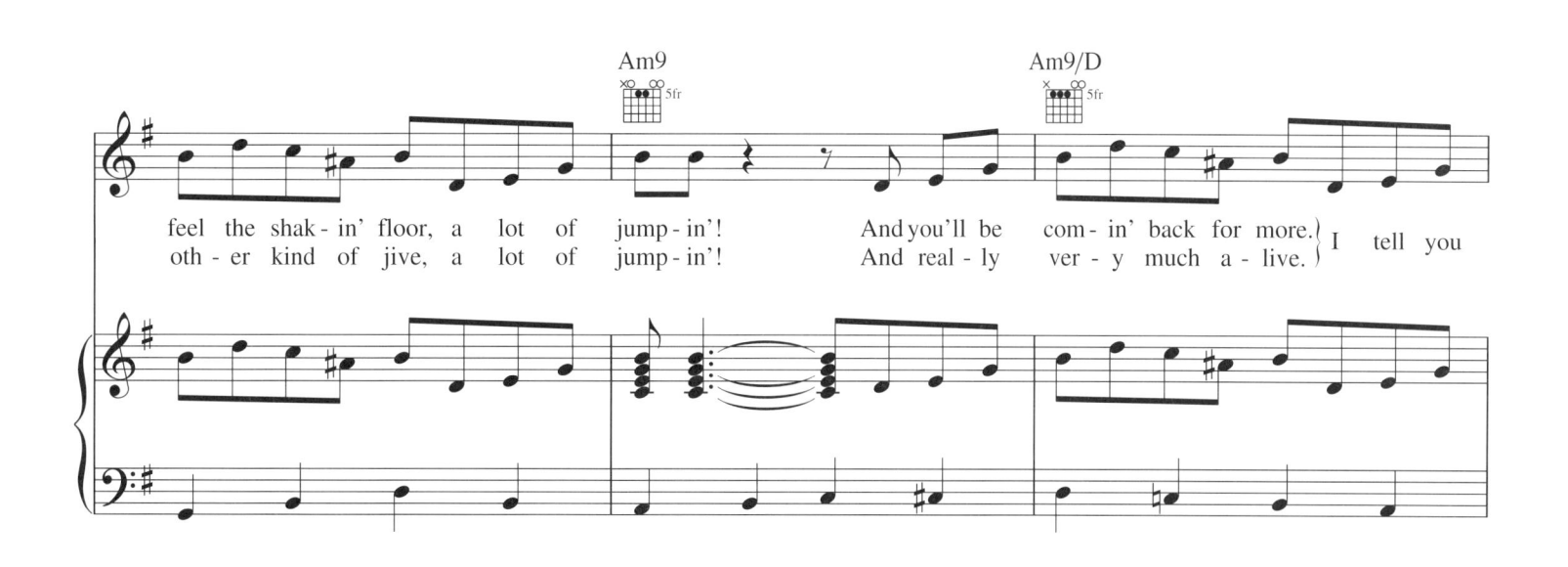

JUST FRIENDS

Lyric by SAM M. LEWIS
Music by JOHN KLENNER

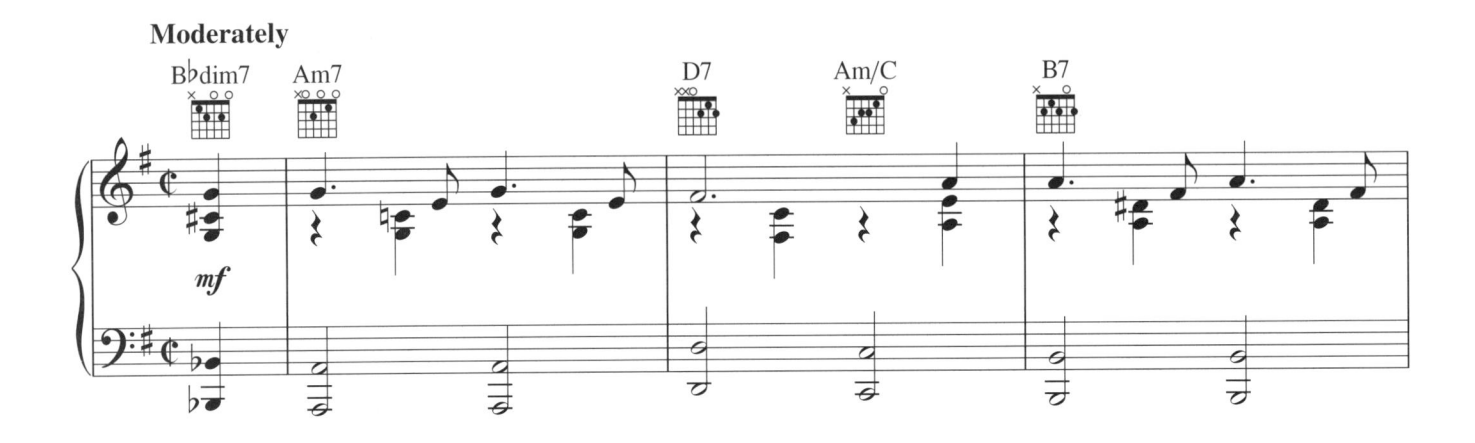

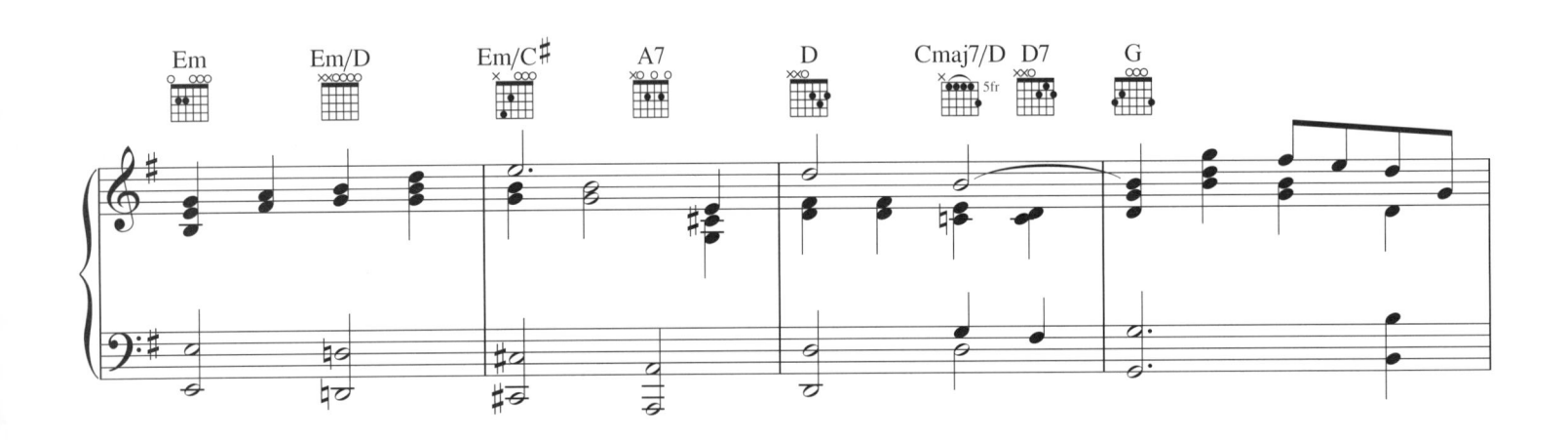

D7 G♯dim7 D7 Gsus G Gdim7
3fr
one with a hand - shake and one with a sigh.
Some - times I won - der if they, too, were lies.
G G6 G+ G/F E7 A9 Em7
3fr
5fr
We two were sweet - hearts by a sa - cred vow.
We who were lov - ers are now on - ly friends.
A7 A6 A7 C/D D7 Ddim7
What are we now? What are we now?
That's how it ends. That's how it ends.
D7 G7 Cmaj7 C6 Cm6
3fr
Just friends, lov - ers no more,
3
3
3
3

just friends _____ but not like be-fore. _____ To think of what we've been and not to kiss a-gain seems like pre-tend-ing. _____ It isn't the end-ing. _____ Two friends _____ drift-ing a-part, two friends but one broken heart. We loved, we laughed, we cried and suddenly love died. The story ends and we're just friends. Just friends.

JUST ONE OF THOSE THINGS
from HIGH SOCIETY

Words and Music by
COLE PORTER

"It was swell, Is-a-belle, swell," _____

As Ab-e-lard _____ said to El-o-ise, _____

_____ "Don't for-get _____ to drop a line to me, please," _____

_____ As Ju-liet cried _____ in her Ro-meo's ear, _____

Cm6/E♭ D7 Gm A7sus A7
"Ro - meo, why not face the fact, my dear?"
Dm A/C♯
It was just one of those things,
A F7 Bm7♭5
Just one of those cra - zy flings.
B♭dim7 F/A Fm/A♭ Gm7
One of those bells that now and then

rings, Just one of those things.

It was just one of those nights,

Just one of those fab-u-lous flights, A trip to the moon on gos-sa-mer wings,

F F♯dim7 Fm7 Fm7/B♭ B♭7
Just one of those things. If we'd
E♭ B♭7
thought a bit of the end of it when we
E♭ 3fr
E♭ G7 C6
start - ed paint - ing the town, We'd have been a - ware
E♭ 3fr
F♯m7♭5 Fm7 Em7 E♭dim7
That our love af - fair Was too hot not to cool
4fr

193

JUST SQUEEZE ME
(But Don't Tease Me)

Words by LEE GAINES
Music by DUKE ELLINGTON

Slowly, but rhythmic

Want you to know I go for your squeez-in'.
Want you to know it real-ly is pleas-in'. Want you to know I

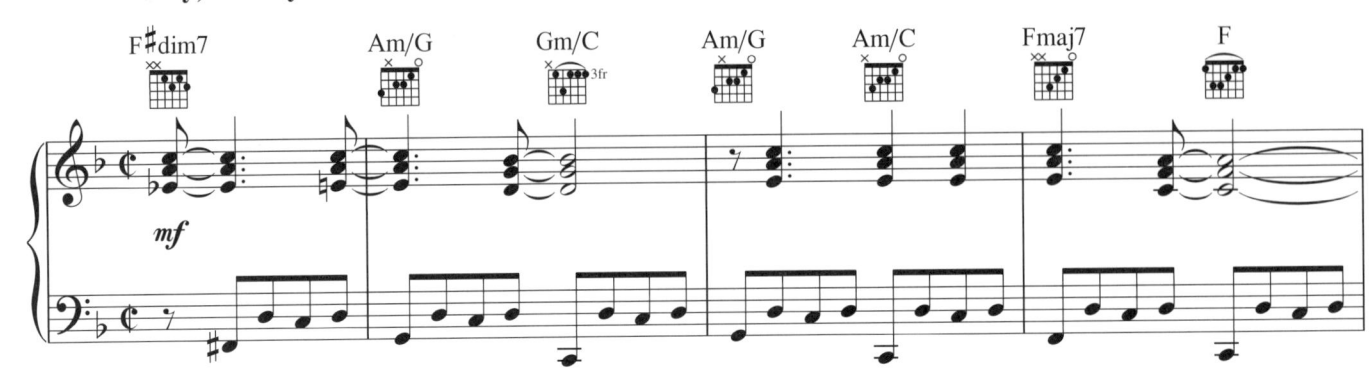

C7 F N.C. G G7♯5 C9
ain't for no teas - in'.
F Gm Fmaj7 F Gm
Treat me sweet and gen - tle when you say good - night.
Fmaj7 F♯dim7 Am/G Gm/C Am/G Am/C
Just squeeze me, but please don't
Fmaj7 F Gm G♯m/C Am/C F Gm
tease me. I get sen - ti - men -

-tal when you hold me tight. Just squeeze me, but please don't tease me.

Missing you since you went away, singing the blues away each day, counting the nights and waiting for you.

G7
Gm7
I'm in the mood to let you know I nev-er knew I loved you so. Please say you
C7
F
Gm
Fmaj7
love me, too. When I get this feel - in',
F
Gm
Fmaj7
F♯dim7
Am/G
Gm/C
Am/G
Am/C
I'm in ec-sta - sy. So squeeze me, but please don't
1
Fmaj7
F
tease me.
2
Fmaj7
F
F6
tease me.

A KISS TO BUILD A DREAM ON

Words and Music by BERT KALMAR,
HARRY RUBY and OSCAR HAMMERSTEIN II

Slowly

Give me a kiss to build a dream on and my i-magi-
Give me a kiss be-fore you leave me and my i-magi-
Give me your lips for just a mo-ment and my i-magi-

na-tion will thrive up-on that kiss. Sweet-heart, I ask no more than
na-tion will feed my hun-gry heart. Leave me one thing be-fore we
na-tion will make that mo-ment live. Give me what you a-lone can

this, a kiss to build a dream on.
part, a kiss to build a
give, a kiss to build a

© 1935 (Renewed) METRO-GOLDWYN-MAYER INC.
All Rights Controlled and Administered by EMI Miller Catalog Inc. (Publishing) and ALFRED MUSIC (Print)
All Rights Reserved   Used by Permission

199

dream on. When I'm a - dream on.

lone with my fan - cies,

I'll be with you, weav - ing ro -

manc - es, mak - ing be - lieve they're true.

THE LAMP IS LOW

Music by PETER DeROSE and BERT SHEFTER
Words by MITCHELL PARISH
Original French Lyrics by YVETTE BARUCH
Melody based on a Theme from Ravel's *Pavane*

Moderate Swing

An-oth-er per-fect day has come to a close. Twelve o'-clock, all is well. And while a

© 1939 (Renewed) EMI Robbins Catalog Inc.
All Rights Administered by EMI Robbins Catalog Inc. (Publishing) and ALFRED MUSIC (Print)
All Rights Reserved Used By Permission

sleep-y world is lost in re-pose, let my heart soft-ly tell you: Dream be-side me in the mid-night glow, the lamp

F6 Am7 Gm7 Fmaj7 Em7♭9 Dm7 D7/F♯ Gm9 C13
is low. Dream
Gm9 C7 Gm9 C13 Gm9 C7
and watch the shad - ows come and
F6 Fmaj9 F6 G13 C9
go, the lamp is low.
F7 Cm7 F7 Cm7 F7 B♭m6/D♭ C7 F7
While you lin - ger in my arms, my

lips will sigh, "I love you so."

Dream the sweetest dream we'll ev-er know. To-night the moon is high, the lamp is low.

LI'L DARLIN'

Music by NEAL HEFTI

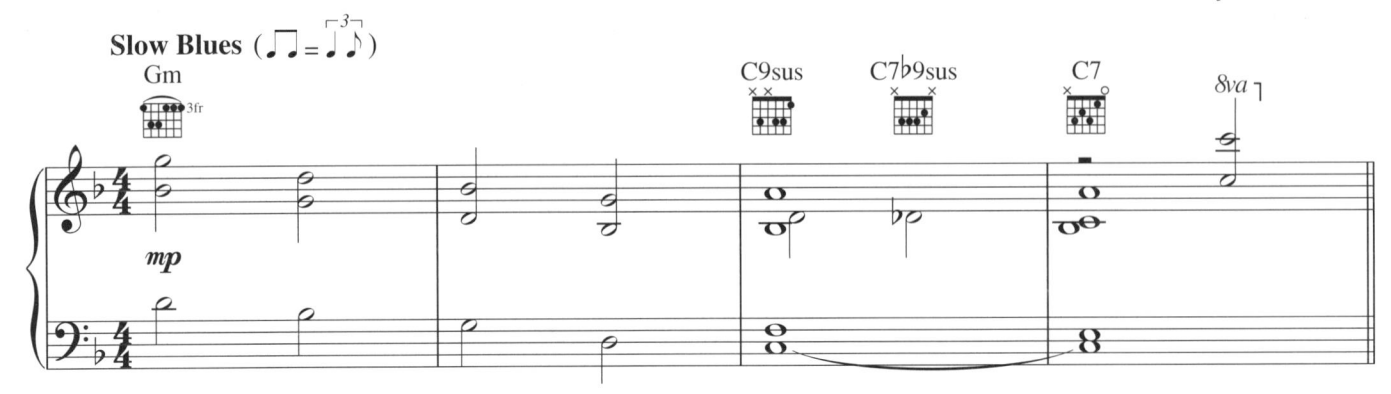

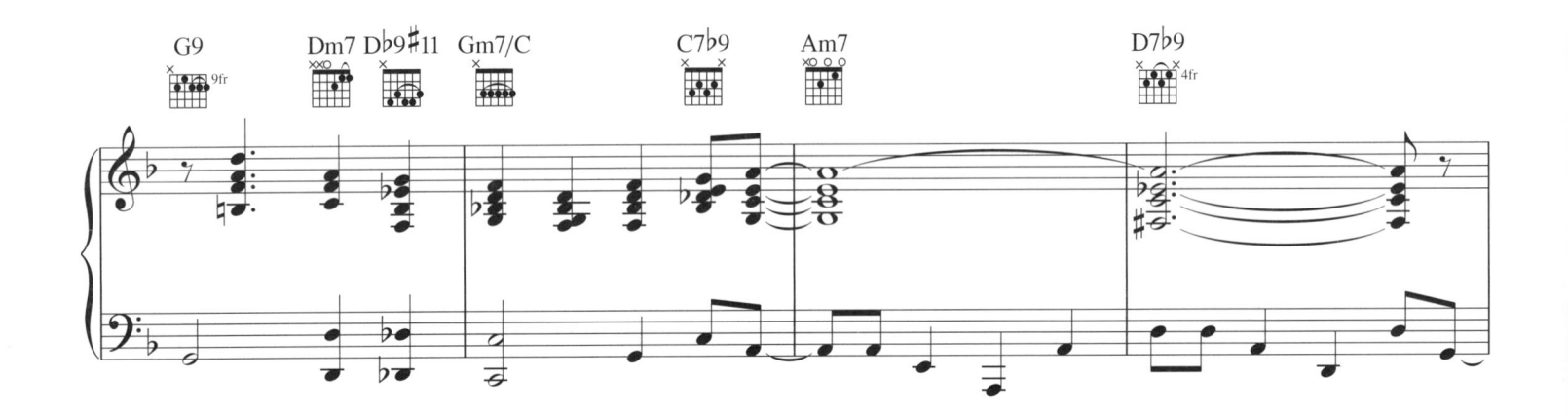

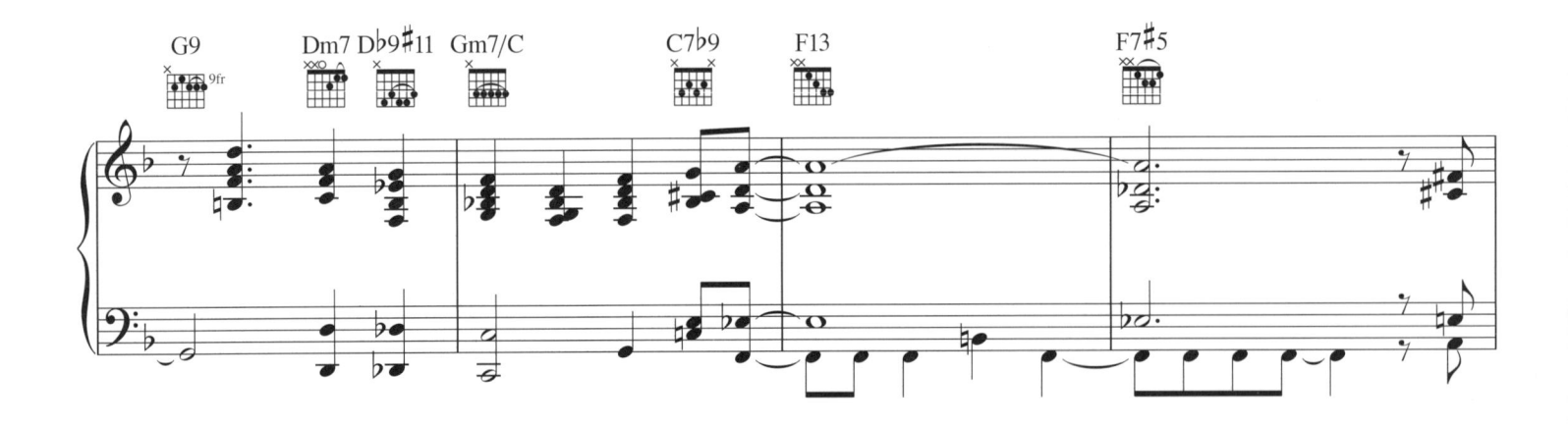

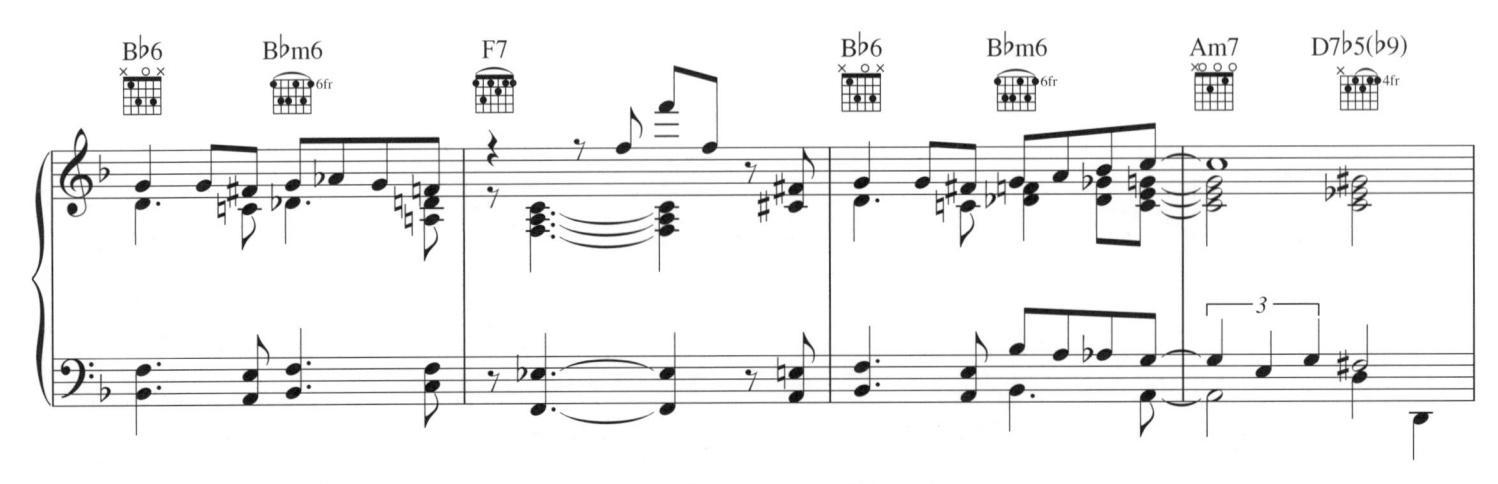

205

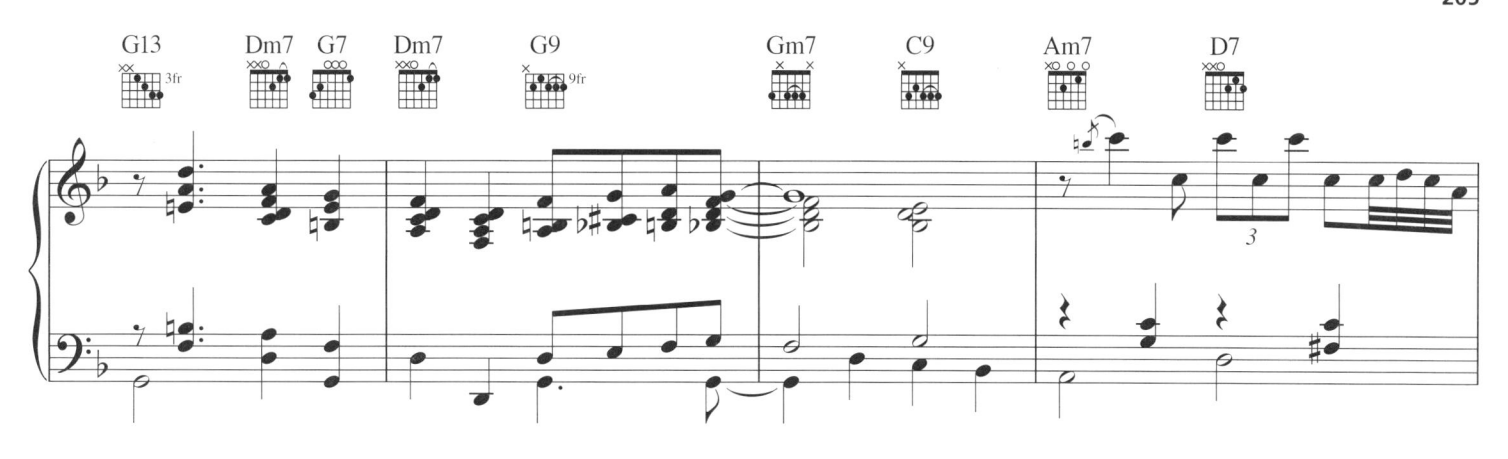

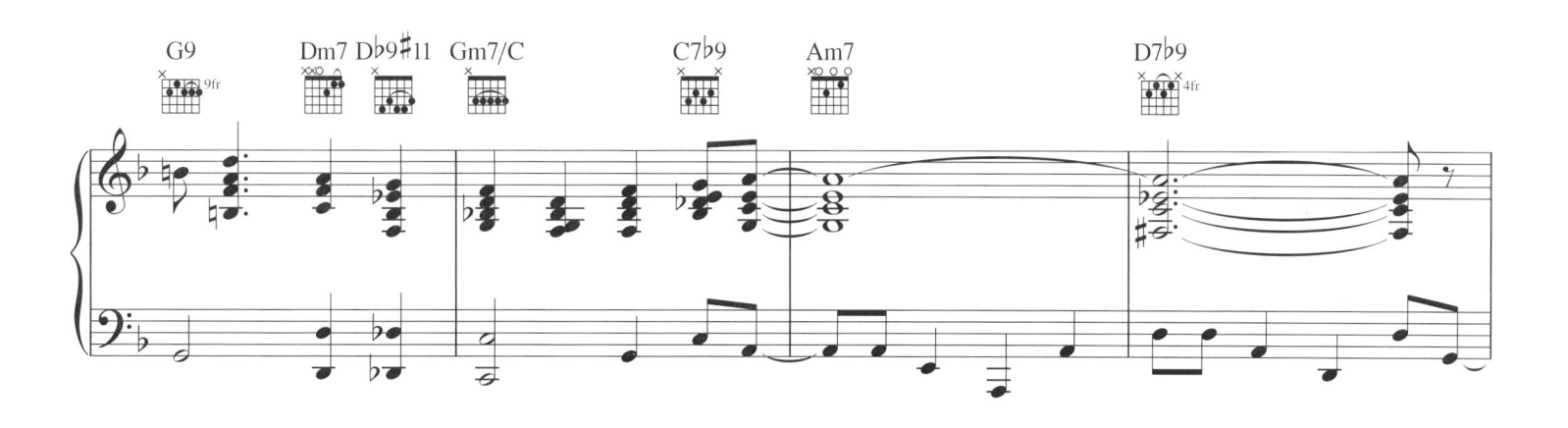

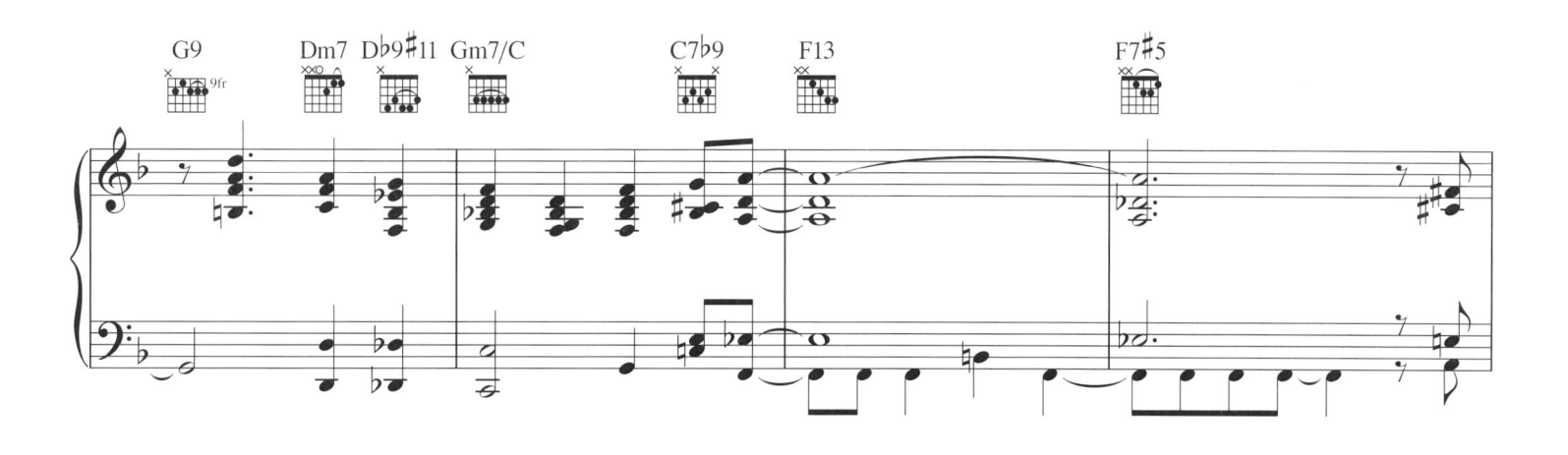

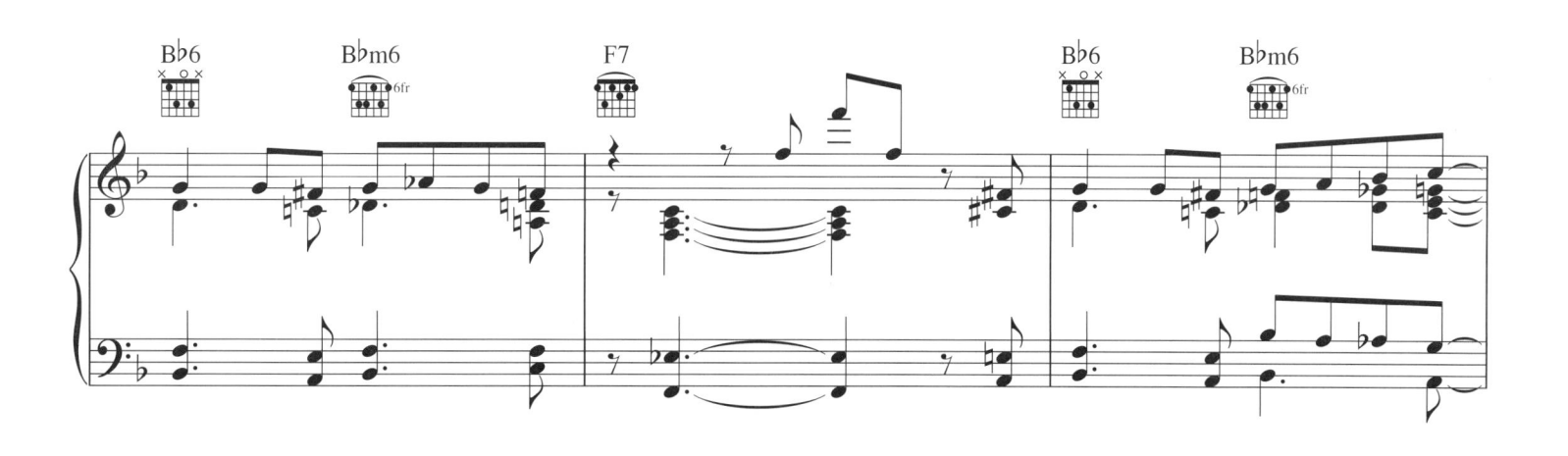

Am7
D7♭5(♭9)
4fr
G9
9fr
Dm7
D♭9♯11
Gm7/C
C7
C7♭9
F6
Am7
D7♭9
4fr
G9
9fr
Dm7
D♭9♯11
Gm7/C
C7
F6
Am7
D7♭9
4fr
G9
9fr
Dm7
D♭9♯11
Gm7/C
C7
C7♭9
F6
E♭m9
4fr
Dm7
D♭maj9
3fr
Gm7/C
Fmaj9
8va
p

LOVE YOU MADLY

By DUKE ELLINGTON

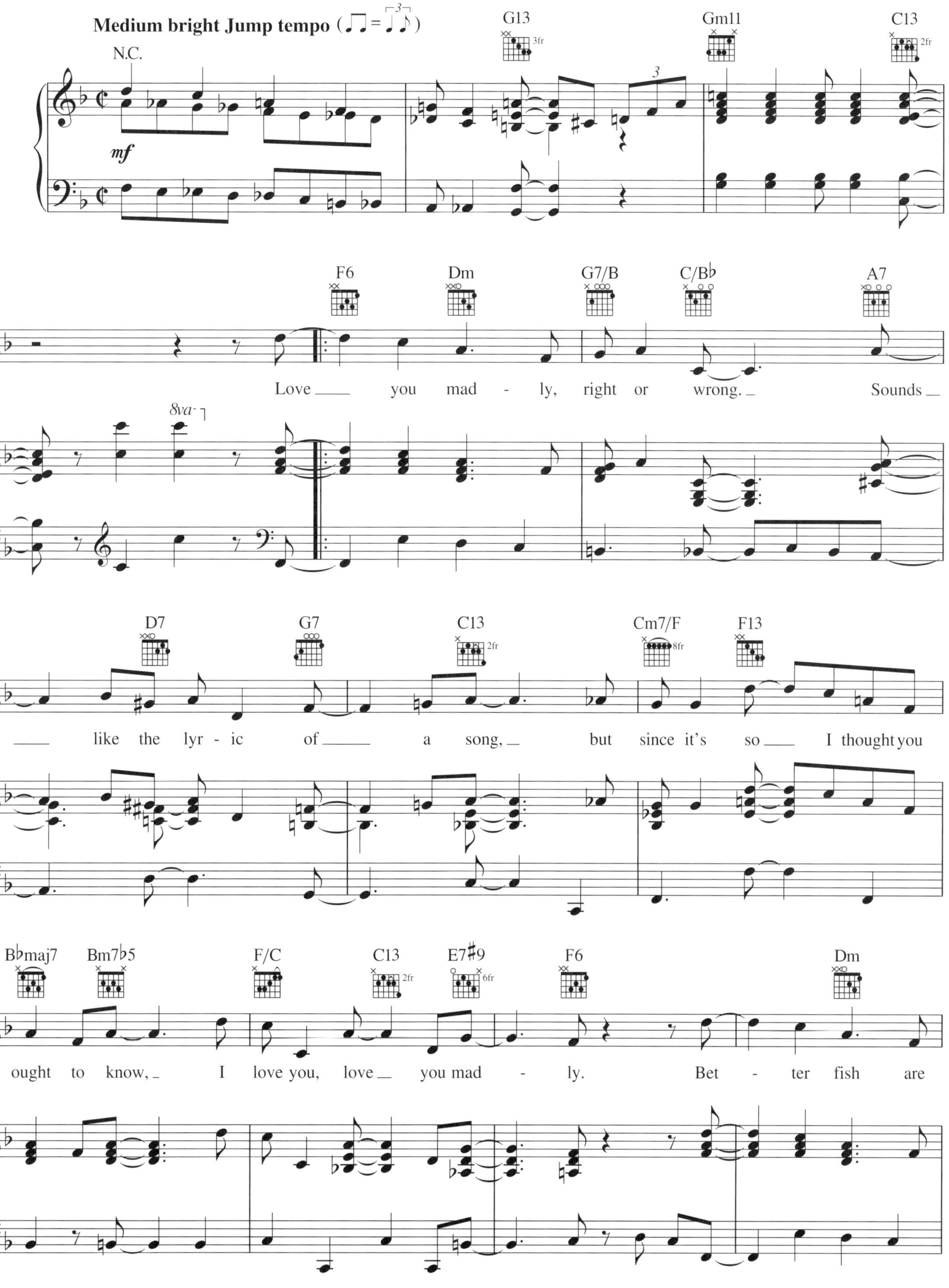

208

lyrics: in the sea is not the the-o-ry for me and that's for sure. Just like I said be-fore, "I love you, love you mad-ly." If you could see the hap-py you and me I dream a-bout so proud-ly, you'd know the breath of spring that makes me sing my love song so loud-ly. Good things come to those who wait, so just re-lax and wait for fate to let me see the day you'll say to me, "I love you, love you mad-ly!" Love-ly!"

LOVE FOR SALE
from THE NEW YORKERS

Words and Music by
COLE PORTER

Moderately

When the on-ly sound in the emp-ty street is the heav-y tread of the heav-y feet that be-long to a lone-some cop, I ____ o-pen shop. When the moon so long has been

© 1930 (Renewed) WB MUSIC CORP.
All Rights Reserved Used by Permission

gaz-ing down on the way-ward ways of this way-ward town that her smile be-comes a smirk, I ____ go to work.

Love ____ for sale, ____ ap-pe-tiz-ing young love for sale. ____

Love that's fresh and still un-spoiled, love that's on-ly slight-ly soiled, love _____ for sale. _____

Who _____ will buy? _____

Who would like to sam-ple my sup-ply? _____

Who's pre-pared to pay the price for a trip to par - a - dise?

Love _____ for sale. _____

Let the po - ets pipe of love in their child - ish way,

I know ev - 'ry type of love bet - ter far then they.

If you want the thrill of love, I've been through the mill of love;
old love, new love, ev-'ry love but true love.

Love for sale, ap-pe-ti-zing young love for sale.

If you want to buy my wares, fol-low me and climb the stairs, love for sale. Love for sale.

LOVE IS HERE TO STAY

from AN AMERICAN IN PARIS
from GOLDWYN FOLLIES

Music and Lyrics by GEORGE GERSHWIN
and IRA GERSHWIN

The more I read the papers The less I comprehend The world and all its capers And how it all will end. Nothing seems to be lasting, But that is-n't our af - fair; We've got some-thing per - ma - nent, I mean in the way we care. It's ver - y clear Our love is here to stay; Not for a year

But ev-er and a day. The ra-di-o and the tel-e-phone and the mov-ies that we know May just be pass-ing fan-cies, And in time may go. But, oh my dear, Our love is here to stay;

Gm7 C7 G7 Gm7/C C7 E♭9 D9
4fr
To - geth - er we're go - ing a long, long way.
G7 C7 D7 Gm7 C7
In time the Rock - ies may crum - ble, Gi - bral - tar may tum - ble,
E♭9 D7 B♭ Bdim7 F/C Gm7 C9
They're on - ly made of clay, But our love is here to
8va
1
F6 C7
stay. It's ver - y
2
F6 C13 F6/9 F
2fr
stay.

LOVE WALKED IN

Music and Lyrics by GEORGE GERSHWIN
and IRA GERSHWIN

Nothing seemed to matter anymore, didn't care what I was headed for. Time was standing still. No one counted

© 1937 (Renewed) GEORGE GERSHWIN MUSIC and IRA GERSHWIN MUSIC
All Rights Administered by WB MUSIC CORP.
All Rights Reserved   Used by Permission

till there came a knock-knock-knocking at the door. Love walked right in and drove the shadows away. Love walked right in and brought my sunniest day. One

E♭+ A♭ A♭6 C7♯5
4fr 3fr 8fr
mag - ic mo - ment and my heart seemed to know
Fm C7 Fm7 E♭ A♭ B♭
3fr 4fr
that love said "Hel - lo," though not a
F9 B♭7 E♭
3fr
word was spo - ken. One look and I for -
F7 B♭7sus B♭7 E♭
3fr
got the gloom of the past. One look and I had

found my future at last. One look and I had found a world completely new when love walked in with you. you.

LUCKY TO BE ME
from ON THE TOWN

Words by BETTY COMDEN and ADOLPH GREEN
Music by LEONARD BERNSTEIN

Freely

GABEY: I used to think it might be fun to be an-y-one else but me.

I thought that it would be a pleas-ant sur-prise to wake up as a cou-ple of

oth-er guys. But now that I've found you I've changed my point of view,

© 1944 (Renewed) WB MUSIC CORP.
All Rights Reserved   Used by Permission

and now I would-n't give a dime to be an-y-one else but me.

rit. e dim. *a tempo*

Gently

What a day, for-tune smiled and came my way, bring-ing love I

nev-er thought I'd see. I'm so luck-y to be me.

What a night, sud-den-ly you came in sight, look-ing just the way I'd hoped you'd be. I'm so luck-y to be me.

I am sim-ply thun-der-struck at the change in my luck.

Knew at once I want-ed you; nev-er dreamed you'd want me, too.

I'm so proud you chose me from all the crowd. There's no oth-er guy I'd rath-er be; I could laugh out loud, I'm so luck-y to be

me.

I am sim-ply thun-der-struck at the change in my luck:

knew at once I want-ed you, nev-er dreamed you'd want me, too.

I'm so proud you chose me from all the crowd,

there's no oth-er guy I'd rath-er be. I could

laugh out loud, I'm so luck-y to be me.

LULLABY OF THE LEAVES

Words by JOE YOUNG
Music by BERNICE PETKERE

A♭7 G7 Cm Fm
in the sun - ny south when I was a tot so
Cm G7 Cm/E♭ Fm/A♭
high. And now that I have grown,
G7 Cm A♭7 G7
and find my - self a - lone:
Cm G7 C7
Cra - dle me where south - ern skies can watch me with a

That's south-land! Don't I feel it in my soul, and don't I know I've reached my goal? Oh, sing me to sleep, lullaby of the leaves. leaves.

LULLABY IN RHYTHM

Words and Music by BENNY GOODMAN,
WALTER HIRSCH, EDGAR SAMPSON
and CLARENCE PROFIT

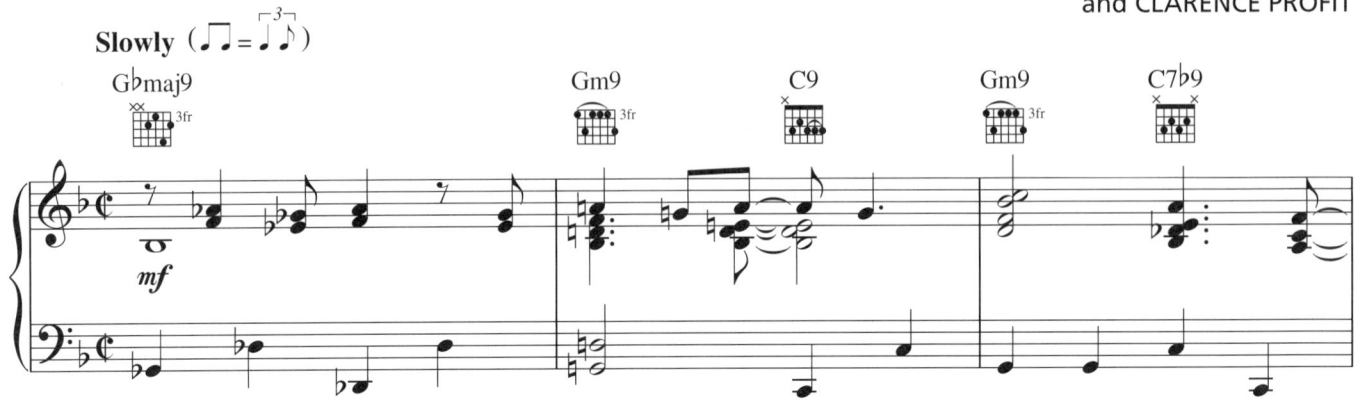

When the day is done __ and the sun is red __ out in the west-ern skies, __ why you lay your head __ in your

Copyright © 1938 (Renewed) by Ragbag Music Publishing Corp. (ASCAP) and EMI Feist Catalog Inc. (ASCAP)
International Copyright Secured   All Rights Reserved
Used by Permission

Am Fm C/G Gdim7 G7 C7
ti - ny bed, and you close your sleep - y eyes:
F C7♭9 F
Hear my lull - a - by in rhy - thm. Dream your dreams and
A♭m7 D♭9 G♭maj9 Gm7 C9
wan - der with 'em. Ev' - ning drums will come and take you
Gm7 C7♭9 F6 F
thru the night. To my lull - a -

by in rhy-thm, all the breez-es sigh in rhy-thm.

Rest, my love; let noth-ing wake you till the light.

Stars dance while the shad-ows creep. The moon man's

goin' to swing you up high, swing you to sleep.

Hear my lull-a-by in rhy-thm. Dream your dreams and wander with 'em. Sand-man's goin' to come and make you sleep, good-night.

MACK THE KNIFE
from THE THREEPENNY OPERA

English Words by MARC BLITZSTEIN
Original German Words by BERT BRECHT
Music by KURT WEILL

Moderately, with a beat

Oh, the shark has pretty teeth, dear, and he shows them pearly white. Just a jack-knife has Mac-heath, dear, and he keeps it out of

© 1928 (Renewed) UNIVERSAL EDITION
© 1955 (Renewed) WEILL-BRECHT-HARMS CO., INC.
Renewal Rights Assigned to the KURT WEILL FOUNDATION FOR MUSIC, Bert Brecht and THE ESTATE OF MARC BLITZSTEIN
All Rights Administered by WB MUSIC CORP.
All Rights Reserved   Used by Permission

C6
G9
C6
Dm
9fr
sight. When the shark bites with his teeth, dear,
Dm7
G9
C6
C
9fr
scar - let bil - lows start to spread. Fan - cy
Am
Am7
Dm7
gloves, though, wears Mac - heath, dear, so there's
G7
C6
G9
9fr
not a trace of red. On the

side - walk ____ Sun - day morn - ing ____ lies a
Mil - ler ____ dis - ap - peared, dear, ____ after

bod - y ____ ooz - ing life; ____ some - one's
draw - ing ____ out his cash; ____ and Mac -

sneak - ing ____ 'round the cor - ner. ____ Is the
heath spends ____ like a sail - or. ____ Did our

some - one ____ Mack the Knife? ____ From a
boy do ____ some - thing rash? ____ Su - key

tug-boat by the river a ce-
Taw-dry, Jenny Diver, Polly
ment bag's dropping down; the ce-
Peach-um, Lucy Brown; oh, the
ment's just for the weight, dear. Bet you Mackie's
line forms on the right, dear, now that Mackie's

back in town. Lou-ie
back in town.

THE MAN I LOVE
from STRIKE UP THE BAND

Music and Lyrics by GEORGE GERSHWIN
and IRA GERSHWIN

When the mel-low moon be-gins to beam, Ev-'ry night I dream a lit-tle dream, And, of course, Prince Charm-ing is the theme, The he for me. Al-though I re-al-ize as well as you,

© 1924 (Renewed) WB MUSIC CORP.
All Rights Reserved   Used by Permission

It is seldom that a dream comes true, To me it's clear That he'll appear.

Slow

Some-day he'll come a-long, The man I love; And he'll be big and strong, The man I love; And when he comes my way, I'll do my best to make him stay. He'll look at me and smile, I'll un-der-stand; And in a lit-tle while He'll take my hand; And though it seems ab-surd, I know we both won't say a word. May-be I shall meet him Sun-day, May-be Mon-day may-be

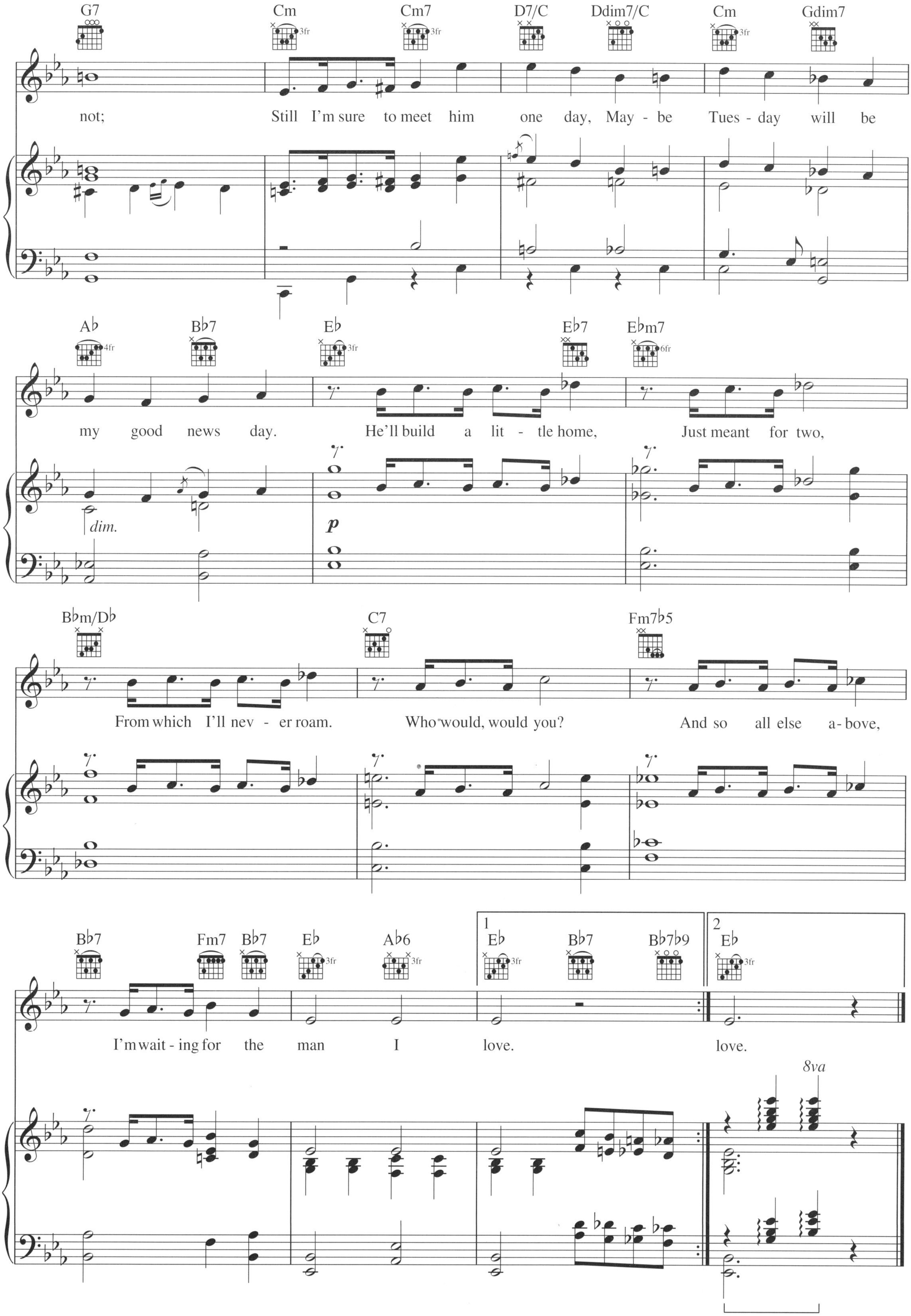

MIDNIGHT SUN

Words and Music by LIONEL HAMPTON,
SONNY BURKE and JOHNNY MERCER

star its own au-ro-ra bo-re-al-is; sud-den-ly you held me tight. I could see the mid-night sun. I can't ex-plain the sil-ver rain that found me, or was that a moon-lit veil? The mu-sic of the u-ni-verse a-round me, or was that a night - in - gale? And then your arms mi-rac-u-lous-ly

found me, sud - den - ly the sky turned pale. I could see the

mid - night sun. Was there such a night? It's a

thrill I still don't quite be - lieve, but

...after you were gone, there was still some stardust on my sleeve.

The flame of it may dwindle to an ember, and the stars forget to shine, and we may see the meadow in December, icy white and crystaline.

But, oh, my darling, always I'll remember when your lips were close to mine and {I/we} saw the midnight sun. Your midnight sun.

THE MORE I SEE YOU

from the Twentieth Century-Fox Technicolor Musical
BILLY ROSE'S DIAMOND HORSESHOE

Words by MACK GORDON
Music by HARRY WARREN

Moderately

Each time I look at you is like the first time. Each time you're near me, the thrill is new. And there is noth-ing that I would-n't do for the rare de-light of the sight of

© 1945 (Renewed) WB MUSIC CORP.
All Rights Reserved   Used by Permission

you. For, _____ the more I see you, _____ the more I want you. _____ Some-how this feel-ing _____ just grows and grows. _____ With ev-'ry sigh I be-come more mad a-bout you; _____ more lost with-out you, _____ and so it goes. _____ Can you imag-ine how much I'll love you, the more I see you as years go by? I know the only one for me can only be you. My arms won't free you, my heart won't try. The more I try. The more I try.

MY ONE AND ONLY LOVE

Words by ROBERT MELLIN
Music by GUY WOOD

The ver-y thought of you makes my heart sing ___ like an A-pril breeze ___ on the wings of spring, and you ap-pear in all your splen-dor, ___ my one and on-ly love. The shad-ows fall and spread their

© 1952, 1953 (Renewed 1980, 1981) EMI MUSIC PUBLISHING LTD. and WAROCK CORP.
All Rights for EMI MUSIC PUBLISHING LTD. Controlled and Administered by Colgems-EMI MUSIC INC.
All Rights Reserved   International Copyright Secured   Used by Permission

mys - tic charms ___ in the hush of night ___ while you're in my arms.

I feel your lips so warm and ten - der, ___ my one and on - ly

love. The touch ___ of your hand ___ is like heav - en, ___ a

heav - en that I've ___ nev - er known. The blush ___ on your cheek when-

A9
5fr
Dm7
Dm7/G
G7♭9
ev - er I speak tells me that you are my own.
C
Em7
Dm7
G9
9fr
Am
Fmaj7
F6
You fill my ea - ger heart with such de - sire. Ev - 'ry kiss you give sets my
Dm6/B
Em7
Dm7
G7
Am
soul on fire. I give my - self in sweet sur - ren - der,
Dm7
G7♯5(♭9)
1
C
E♭dim7
Dm7
G7♯5(♭9)
2
A♭maj7
D♭6
C6/9
my one and on - ly love. love.

NICE WORK IF YOU CAN GET IT
from A DAMSEL IN DISTRESS

Music and Lyrics by GEORGE GERSHWIN
and IRA GERSHWIN

one girl, sighing sigh after sigh,

nice work if you can get it, and you can get it if you try.

Just imagine someone

waiting at the cottage door, where two hearts be-come one. Who could ask for an-y-thing more? Lov-ing one who loves you and then tak-ing that vow, nice work if you can get it, and you can get it. Won't you tell me how?

NIGHT AND DAY
from GAY DIVORCE

Words and Music by
COLE PORTER

Moderately

Like the beat, beat, beat of the tom-tom; When the jun-gle shad-ows fall, Like the tick, tick, tock of the state-ly clock, as it stands a-gainst the wall, Like the drip, drip, drip of the rain-drops, When the sum-mer show'r is

© 1934 (Renewed) WB MUSIC CORP.
All Rights Reserved   Used by Permission

through; So a voice with-in me keeps re-peat-ing, you, you, you. Night and day

you are the one, _____ On-ly you _____

be-neath the moon and un-der the sun. _____ Wheth-er near to me or

far, _____ It's no mat-ter, dar-ling, where you are _____ I think of you _____

B♭7 E♭ Bmaj7 B♭7 B♭+
night and day. Day and night Why is it
E♭maj7 E♭6 Bmaj7 B♭7 B♭7♯5 E♭maj7
so, That this long - ing for you fol-lows wher-ev-er I go?
E♭6 Am7♭5 A♭m7 Gm7 G♭dim7
In the roar-ing traf-fic's boom In the si-lence of my lone-ly room, I
Fm7 B♭7sus/F B♭7 E♭ E♭/G G♭
think of you, night and day. Night and day
mf espr.

under the hide of me ____ There's an Oh, such a hungry yearning, burning inside of me. ____ And its torment won't be through ____ 'Til you let me spend my life making love to you, day and night, ____ night and day. ____ Night and day ____

A NIGHTINGALE SANG IN BERKELEY SQUARE

Lyric by ERIC MASCHWITZ
Music by MANNING SHERWIN

When true lov-ers meet in May-fair, so the leg-ends tell, song-birds sing, win-ter turns to spring, ev-'ry wind-ing street in May-fair falls be-neath the spell. I know such en-chant-ment can be, 'cause it hap-pened one eve-ning to me. That cer-tain night, the night we met, there was magic a-broad in the air. There were an-gels din-ing at the Ritz, and a night-in-gale sang in *Ber-k'ley Square.

strange it was, how sweet and strange. There was nev-er a dream to com-pare with that ha-zy, cra-zy night we met, when a night-in-gale sang in Ber-k'ley Square.

*Pronounced "Bar-kley"

I may be right, I may be wrong, but I'm
This heart of mine beat loud and fast like a

per-fect-ly will-ing to swear, that when you turned and
mer-ry-go-round in a fair, for we were danc-ing

smiled at me a night-in-gale sang in Ber-k'ley
cheek to cheek and a night-in-gale sang in Ber-k'ley

Square. The moon that lin-gered o-ver
Square. When dawn came steal-ing up all

| Am7 | D7 | Bm7 | B♭dim7 | Am7 | D7 |

Lon - don town, __ poor puz - zled moon, he wore a frown.
gold and blue __ to in - ter - rupt our ren - dez - vous,

| G | Em7 | Am7 | D7 |

How could he know we two were so in love? __ The
I still re - mem - ber how you smiled and said, __ "Was

| Bm7 | Edim | Fm7 | B♭7 | E♭ | Cm |

whole darn world seemed up - side down. The streets of town were
that a dream or was it true?" Our home - ward step was

| Gm | E♭7 | A♭ | G7 | Cm | A♭m6/C♭ |

paved with stars; it was such a ro - man - tic af - fair. And
just as light as the tap - danc - ing feet of As - taire. And

E♭ B♭7 E♭7 Fm7♭5 E♭/B♭ Cm
as we kissed and said "good - night," a night - in - gale sang in
like an ech - o far a - way, a night - in - gale sang in
Fm7 B♭7 E♭ Cm Fm7 B♭7
1
Ber - k'ley Square. How
Ber - k'ley
2
E♭ Cm Fm7 B♭7 B♭m6/D♭ C7
Square. I know 'cause I was there
Fm7♭5 A♭/B♭ B♭7 E♭ Cm A♭m6 E♭
that night in Ber - k'ley Square.
rall.

OVER THE RAINBOW

from THE WIZARD OF OZ

Music by HAROLD ARLEN
Lyric by E.Y. "YIP" HARBURG

When all the clouds darken up the sky-way, there's a rainbow highway to be found, leading from your window-pane to a place behind the sun, just a step beyond the rain.

rall.

E♭6 Cm7 Gm E♭7 A♭ A♭maj7 A♭7 Gm7 Gdim
Some - where o - ver the rain - bow way up high,
p - mf
a tempo
A♭6 A♭m6 E♭/B♭ C7♭9 F7 Fm/B♭ B♭7
there's a land that I heard of once in a lull - a -
E♭ Fm7 B♭7♭9 E♭6 Cm7 Gm E♭7
by. Some - where o - ver the rain - bow
A♭ A♭maj7 A♭7 Gm7 Gdim A♭6 A♭m6 E♭/B♭ C7♭9
skies are blue, and the dreams that you dare to

F7 Fm/B♭ B♭7 E♭
dreamily
dream real - ly do come true. Some - day I'll wish up - on a star and
Fm/E♭ B♭7/E♭ E♭6 B♭/E♭ A♭/E♭ E♭ B♭7/E♭
wake up where the clouds are far be - hind me. Where
E♭ F♯dim Fm6 F7♭9
trou - bles melt like lem - on drops a - way a - bove the chim - ney tops, that's where you'll
Fm7/B♭ B♭9♯5 E♭6 Cm7 Gm E♭7 A♭ A♭maj7 A♭7
find me. Some - where o - ver the rain - bow blue - birds

Gm7 Gdim A♭6 A♭m6 E♭/B♭ C7♭9 F7 Fm/B♭ B♭7
fly. Birds fly o - ver the rain - bow, why then, oh why can't
1 E♭ B♭9 B♭7♭9
I?
2 E♭6 E♭
I?
rall.
Fm7/E♭ E♭ Fm7 B♭7
If
E♭ Fm7 B♭7/F E♭6
hap - py lit - tle blue - birds fly be - yond the rain - bow, why oh why can't I?
rit.
L.H.

NUAGES

By DJANGO REINHARDT
and JACQUES LARUE

Moderate Swing

275

OH, LADY BE GOOD!
from LADY, BE GOOD!

Music and Lyrics by GEORGE GERSHWIN and IRA GERSHWIN

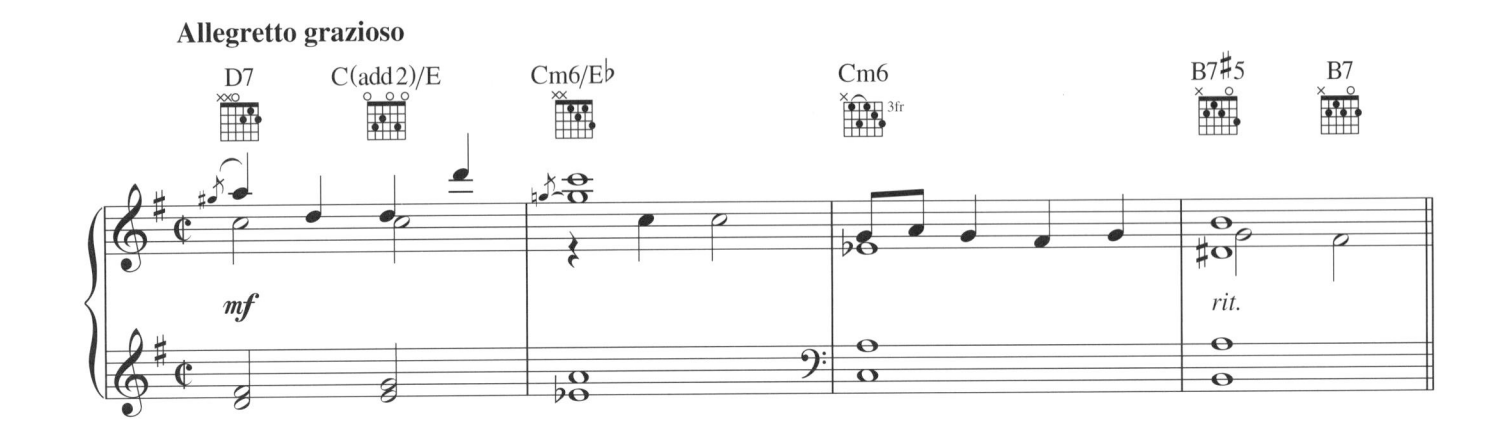

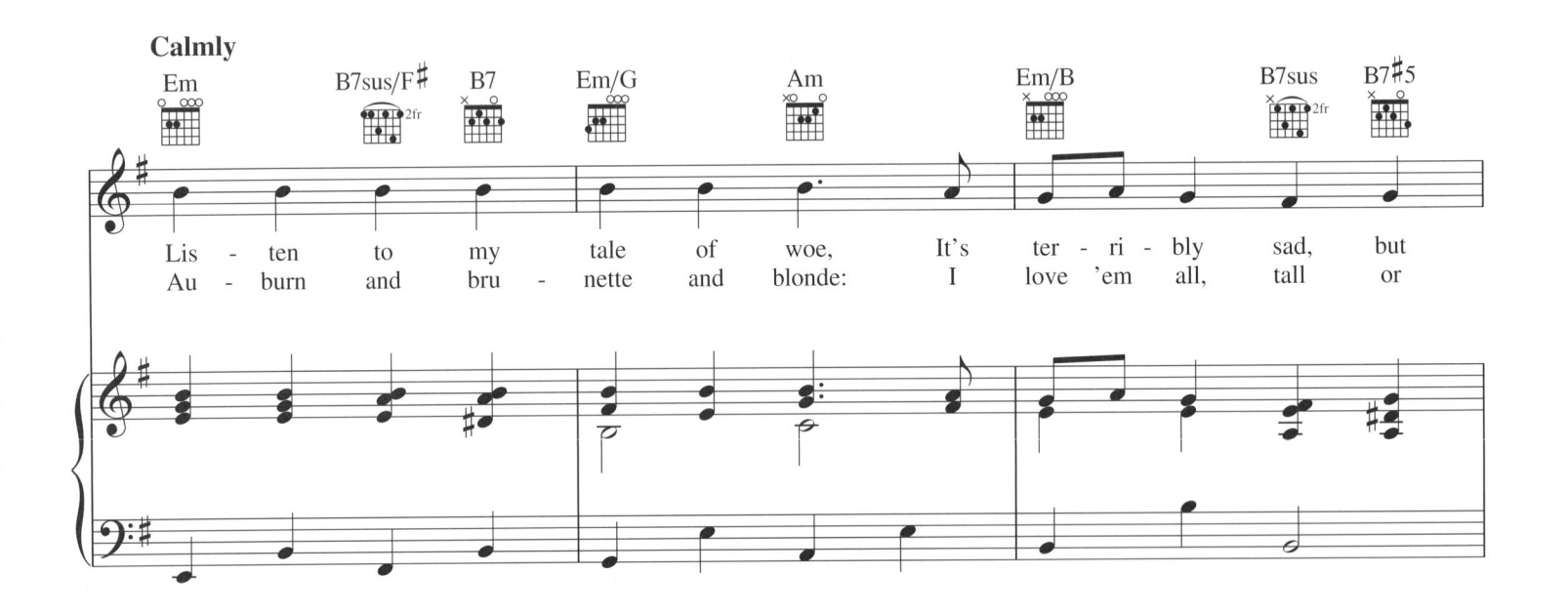

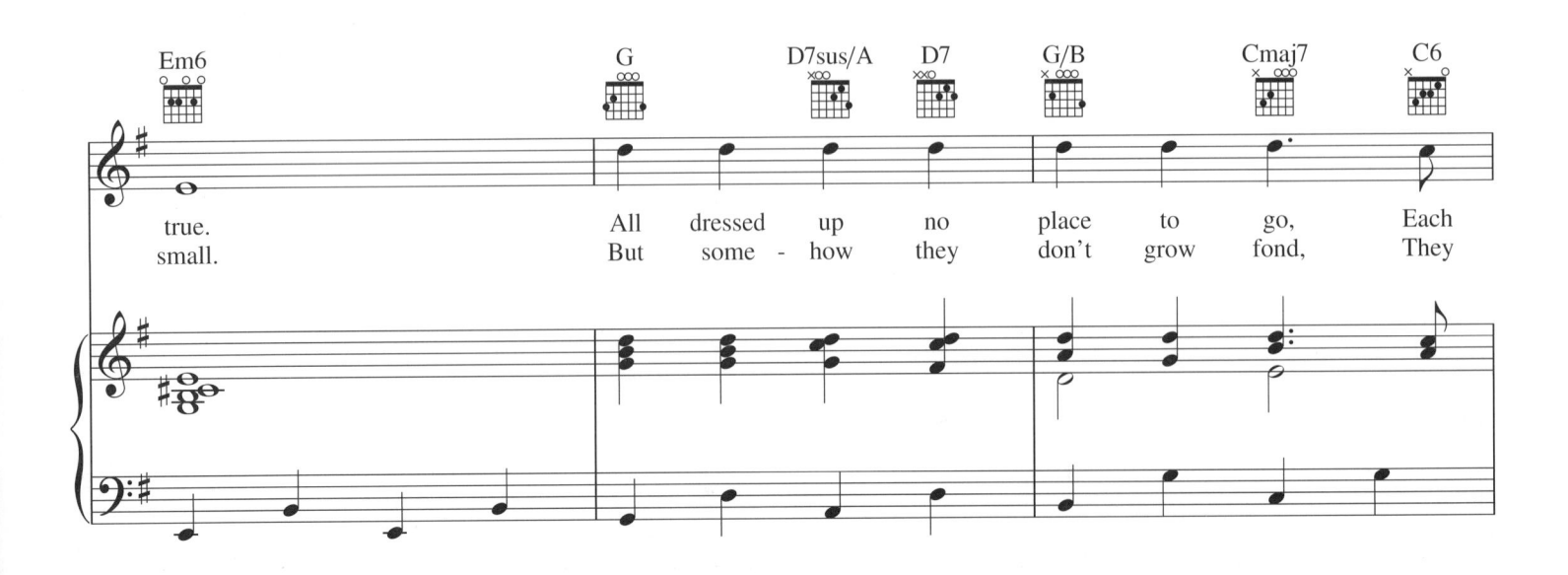

Allegretto grazioso

Calmly

Lis- ten to my tale of woe, It's ter-ri-bly sad, but true.
Au-burn and bru-nette and blonde: I love 'em all, tall or small.

All dressed up no place to go, Each
But some- how they don't grow fond, They

© 1924 (Renewed) WB MUSIC CORP.
All Rights Reserved Used by Permission

ev-'ning I'm aw-f'ly blue. I must win some
stag-ger but nev-er fall. Win-ter's gone, and

win-some miss; Can't go on like this. I could blos-som
now it's Spring! Love! where is thy sting? If some-bod-y

out I know, With some-bod-y just like you. So,
won't re-spond, I'm go-ing to just end it all. So,

Slow and gracefully

Oh, sweet and love-ly la-dy, be good! Oh,
Oh, sweet and love-ly la-dy, be good! Oh,

D7
G
la - dy, be good to me!
la - dy, be good to me!
D7(no3) G C9
G
G♯dim7
I am so aw - f'ly mis - un - der - stood, So,
I am so aw - f'ly mis - un - der - stood, So,
D7
G
G9
9fr
la - dy, be good to me!
la - dy, be good to me!
C C/B D9
4fr
C/G G
N.C.
Oh, please have some pit - y,
This is tu - lip weath - er

I'm all alone in this big cit - y.
So let's put two and two to - geth - er.

I tell you I'm just a lone - some babe in the wood,
I tell you I'm just a lone - some babe in the wood,

So, la - dy, be good to me!
So, la - dy, be good to

me!

OLEO

By SONNY ROLLINS

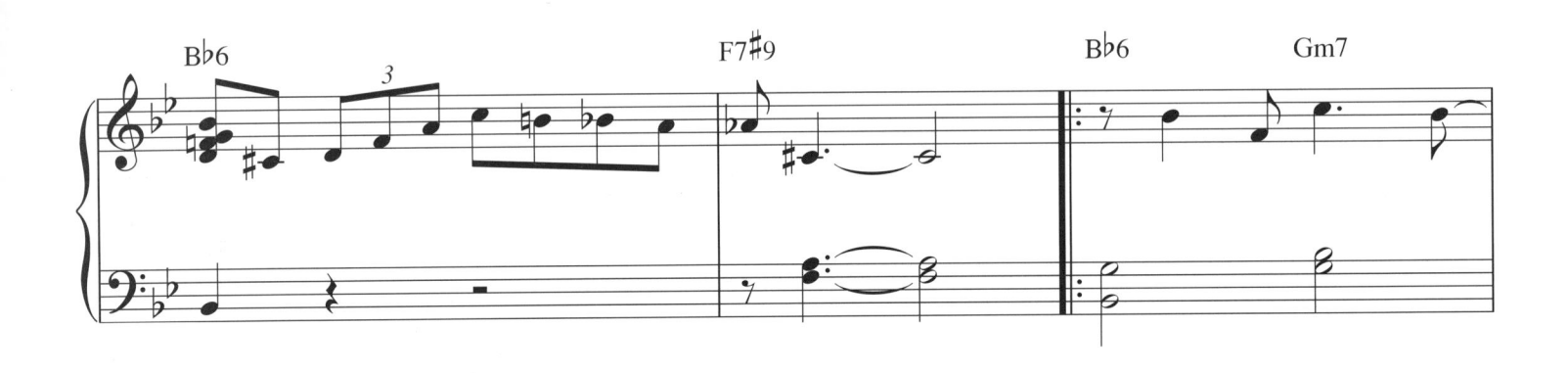

Fm7
B♭7
E♭maj7
Edim7
B♭/F
D♭7
1
Cm7
B7
2
Cm7
F7
B♭6
D7
G7
3
C7
F7
3
B7♭5
B♭6
Gm7
Cm7
F7

Dm7
G7
Cm7
F7
Fm7
B♭7
E♭maj7
Edim7
B♭/F
D♭7
Cm7
F7
B♭
D7
G7
C7
F7
B9
B♭6
Gm7

Cm7
F7
Dm7
G7
Cm7
F7
Fm7
B♭7
E♭maj7
Edim7
B♭/F
D♭7
Cm7
F7
B♭
F7♯9
F7♭9
B♭6
B♭9♯11

ON GREEN DOLPHIN STREET

Lyrics by NED WASHINGTON
Music by BRONISLAU KAPER

It seems like a dream, _____ Yet I know it hap-pened. _____ A man, a maid, a kiss, and then good-bye. _____ Ro-mance was the theme _____ And we were the play-ers, _____

© 1947 (Renewed) Catharine Hinen Music, Patti Washington Music and Primary Wave Songs
All Rights for Primary Wave Songs Controlled by EMI APRIL MUSIC INC. (Publishing) and ALFRED MUSIC (Print)
All Rights Reserved   Used by Permission

Lyrics:
I never think of this without a sigh.

Lover, one lovely day Love came, planning to stay. Green Dolphin Street supplied the set - ting ____ The set - ting for nights be - yond for - get - ting. ____ And through these ____ mo - ments a - part ____ mem - 'ries ____ live in my

C
Dm7
heart.
When I re -
G7
E7
Am
D7
call the love I found on, I could kiss the
C
Gdim7
Dm7
G7
G7♯5
1
C
ground on Green Dol - phin Street.
Dm7
G7
2
C
F
Dm7♭5
Cmaj9
Street.

ONE O'CLOCK JUMP

By COUNT BASIE

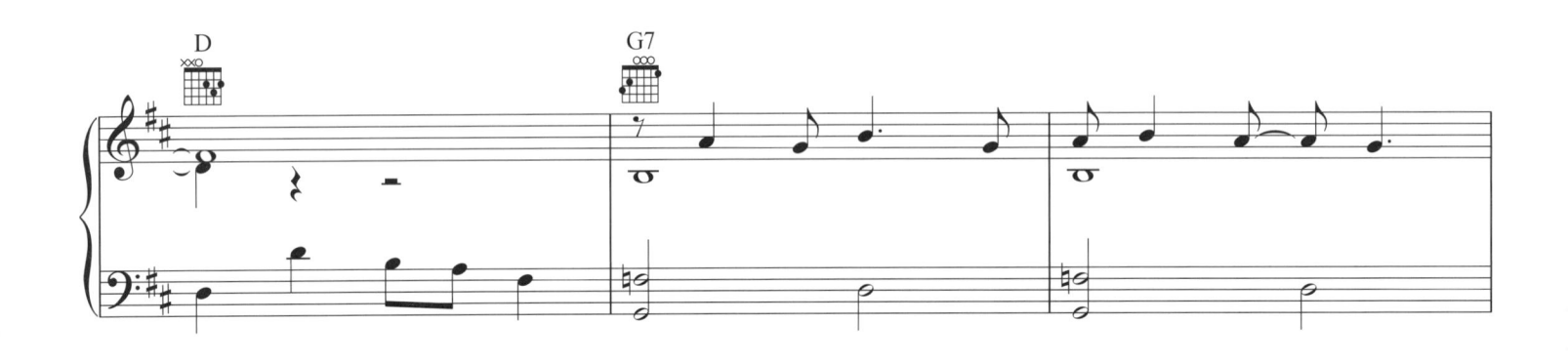

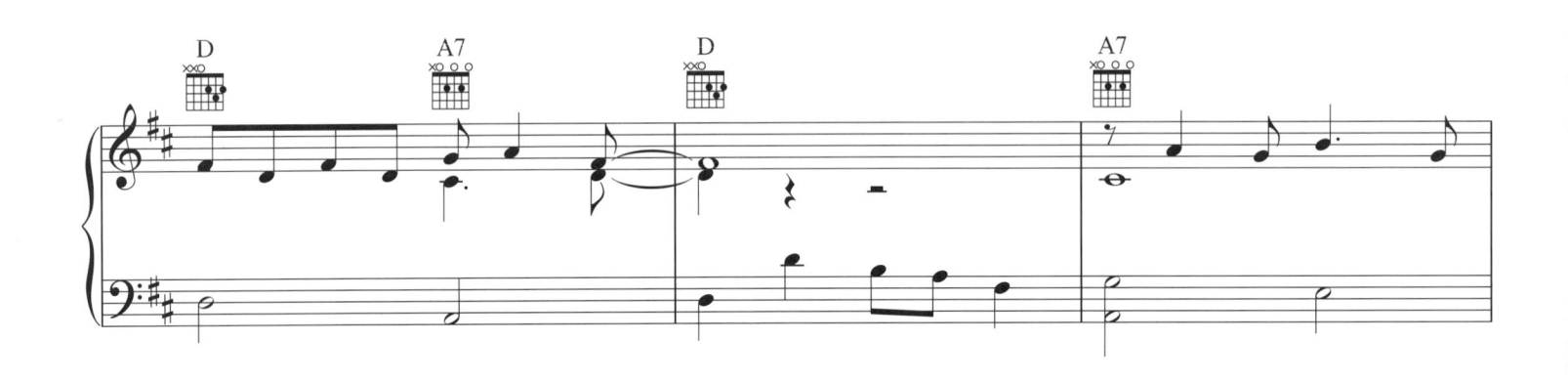

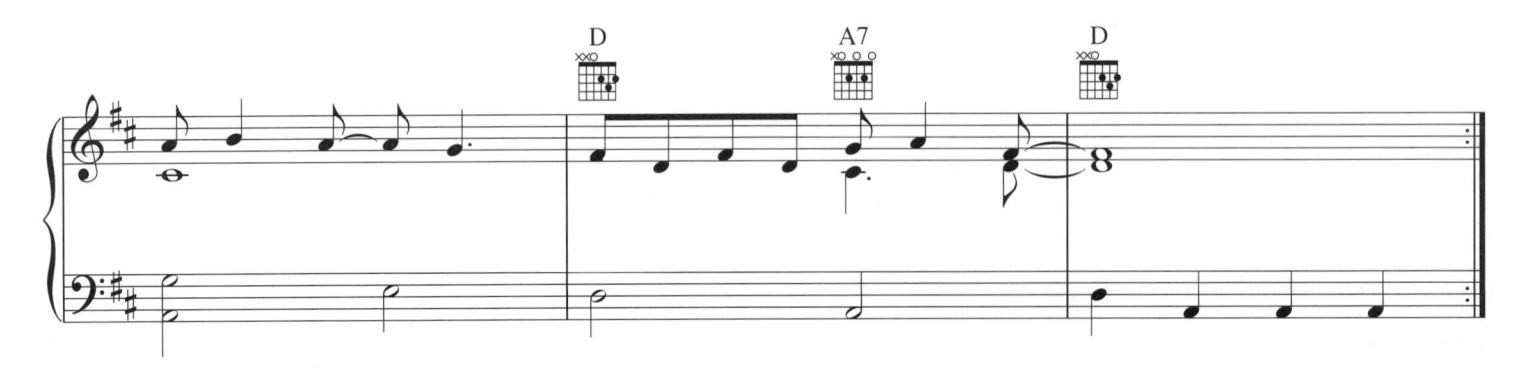

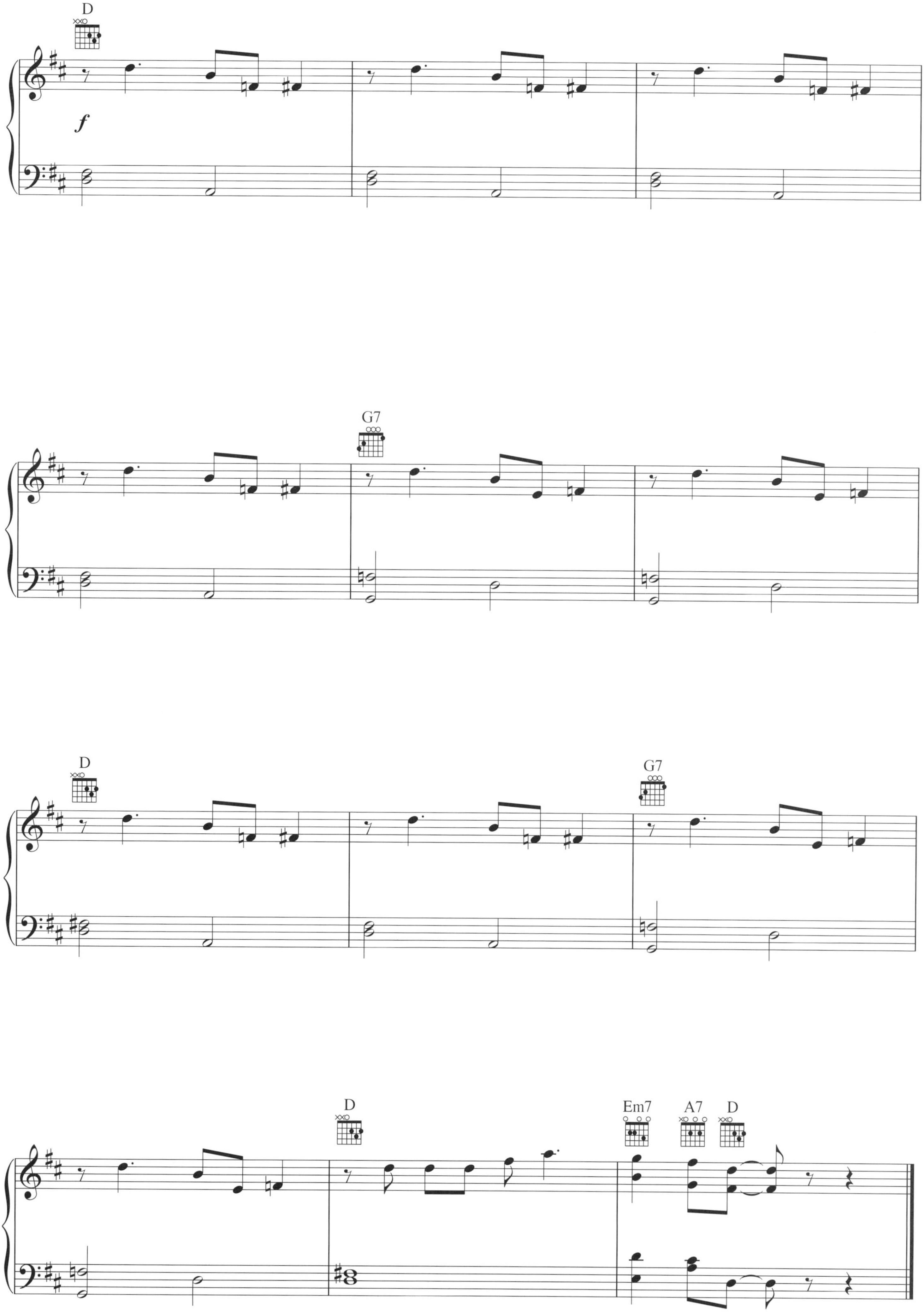
D
f
G7
D
G7
D
Em7
A7
D

PRELUDE TO A KISS

Words by IRVING GORDON and IRVING MILLS
Music by DUKE ELLINGTON

Dm7 G7#5(b9) C6 A7#5(b9) D9 G9#5
my pre - lude to a kiss. If you hear a
C9 Fmaj7 B7b9 E7 A7b9 Dm
song that grows from my ten - der sen - ti - men - tal woes,
Dm7 G7#5 C6 D13 Dm7 G7#5 C6
that was my heart try - ing to com - pose a pre - lude to a kiss.
Emaj7 C#m7 F#m7 B7 Emaj7 C#m7
Though it's just a sim - ple mel - o - dy with noth - ing fan - cy,

F♯m7
Emaj7
C♯m7
F♯m7
B7
E
Edim7
D9
noth-ing much, you could turn it to a sym-pho-ny, a Schu-bert tune with a
G7sus
E♭7sus
D7sus
E9♯11
A7♯5(♭9)
D9
G9♯5
C9
Fmaj7
Gersh - win touch. Oh! How my love song gen - tly cries for the
B7♭9
E7
A7♭9
Dm
Dm7
G7♯5
C6
D13
ten - der - ness with - in your eyes. My love is a pre - lude that nev - er dies,
Dm7
G7♯5(♭9)
C
Fmaj7
E9♯11
A7♯5
C
C6
a pre - lude to a kiss.

REUNION BLUES

By MILT JACKSON

Medium Swing

B♭7sus
Fm7
D7♭5(♯9)
4fr
N.C.
8vb
G7♯5(♭9)
C7♯5(♯9)
2fr
G♭6/9
8fr
F7
F7/A
3fr
B♭7
Bdim
F7/C
3fr
F7
B13
7fr
B♭7
B♭7/C
B♭7/C♯
3fr
B♭7/D
B♭7/E♭
6fr
B♭7/E

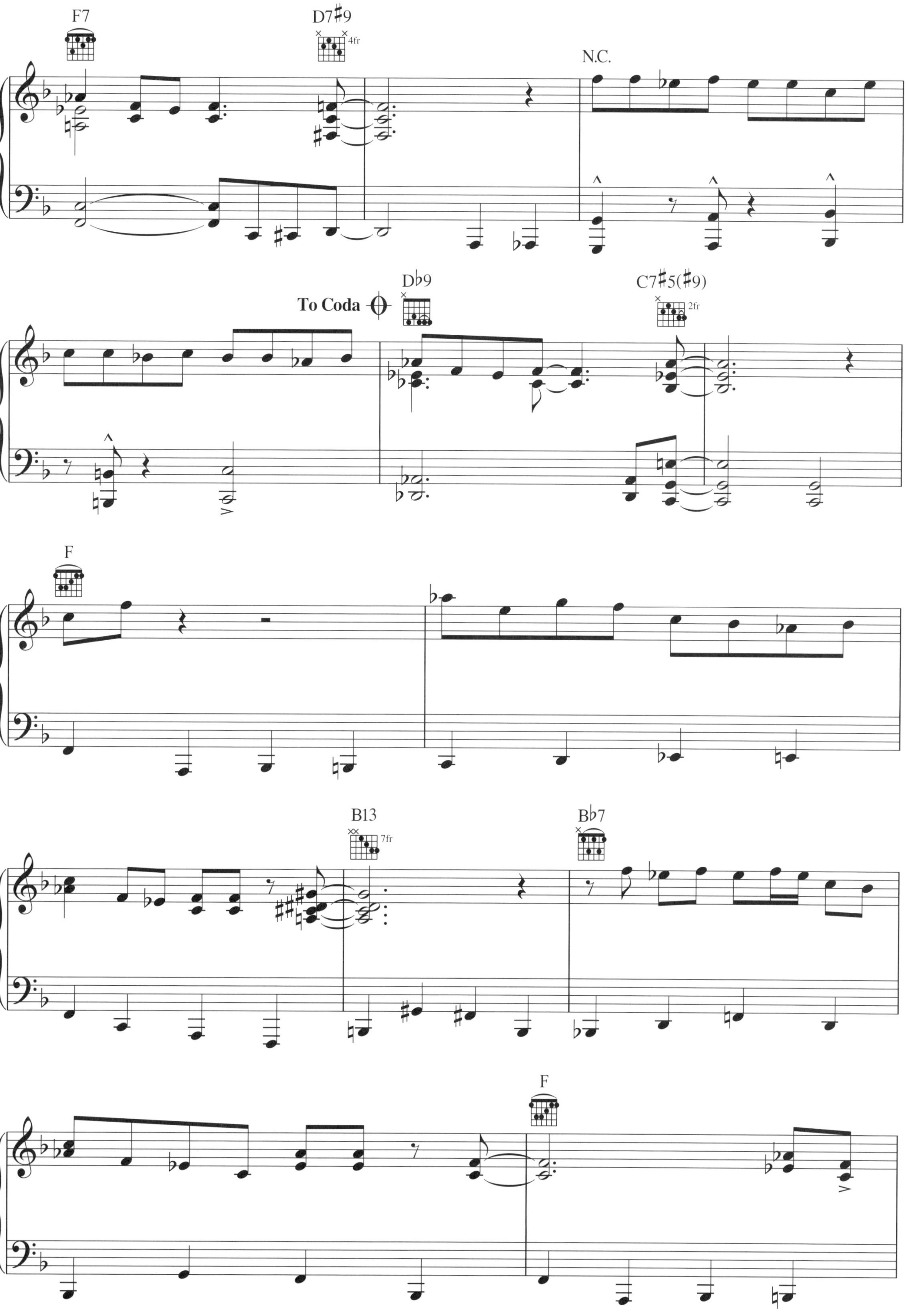
F7
D7♯9
4fr
N.C.
To Coda
D♭9
C7♯5(♯9)
2fr
F
B13
7fr
B♭7
F

Gm7
C7sus
F
D7♯9
A♭13
G13
D♭7♯9
C7♯9
F
Em7♭5
A7
Dm7
G7♭9
Cm7
F7
B♭
B♭m11
Am9
D7♯5(♭9)

A♭m9
4fr
D♭7
4fr
3
Gm7
C7
D.S. al Coda
F
Dm
G7sus
C7sus
CODA
C7sus
D♭maj7
C7sus
D♭maj7
N.C.
G♭6/9
8fr
F6
F13♯11

'ROUND MIDNIGHT

Words by BERNIE HANIGHEN
Music by THELONIOUS MONK
and COOTIE WILLIAMS

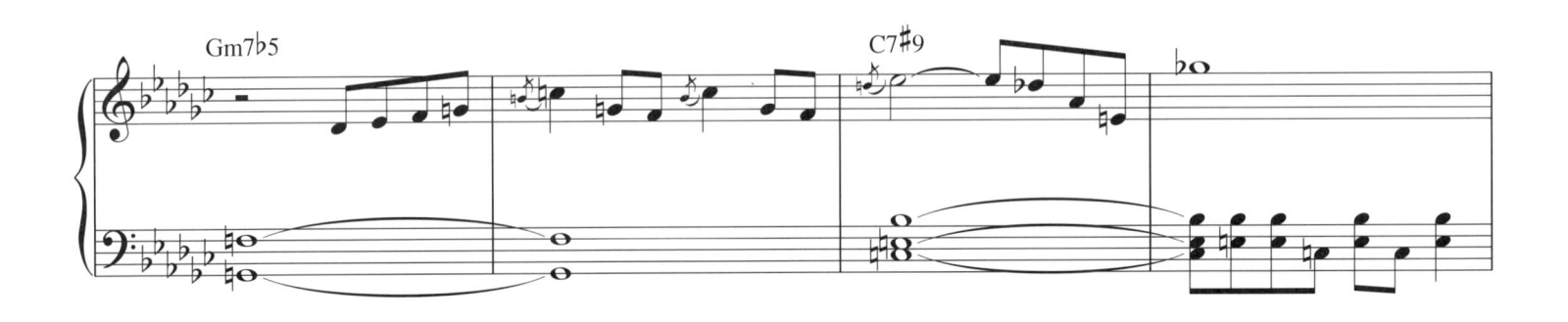

Moderately slow, in 2

E♭m E♭m/D E♭m/D♭ Cm7♭5 Fm7♭5 F♭9
It be - gins to tell 'round mid - night, 'round mid - night.
E♭m E♭m/D Cm7♭5 Bm9 E7(add13) B♭m9 E♭7(add13)
I do pret - ty well till af - ter sun - down.
A♭m7 D♭9 F♭7 E♭m9 A♭9
Sup - per - time, I'm feel - ing sad. But it
Cm7♭5 F7♯4(♯5) C♭9 B♭9 F♭7♭5
real - ly gets bad 'round mid - night.

Mem-'ries al-ways start 'round mid-night, 'round mid-night.

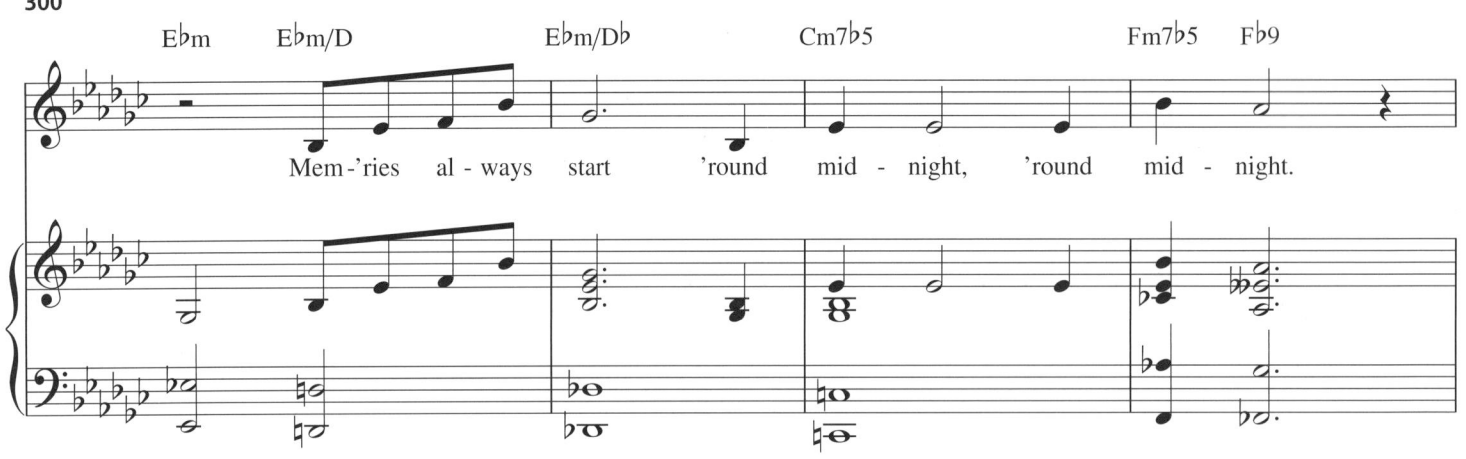

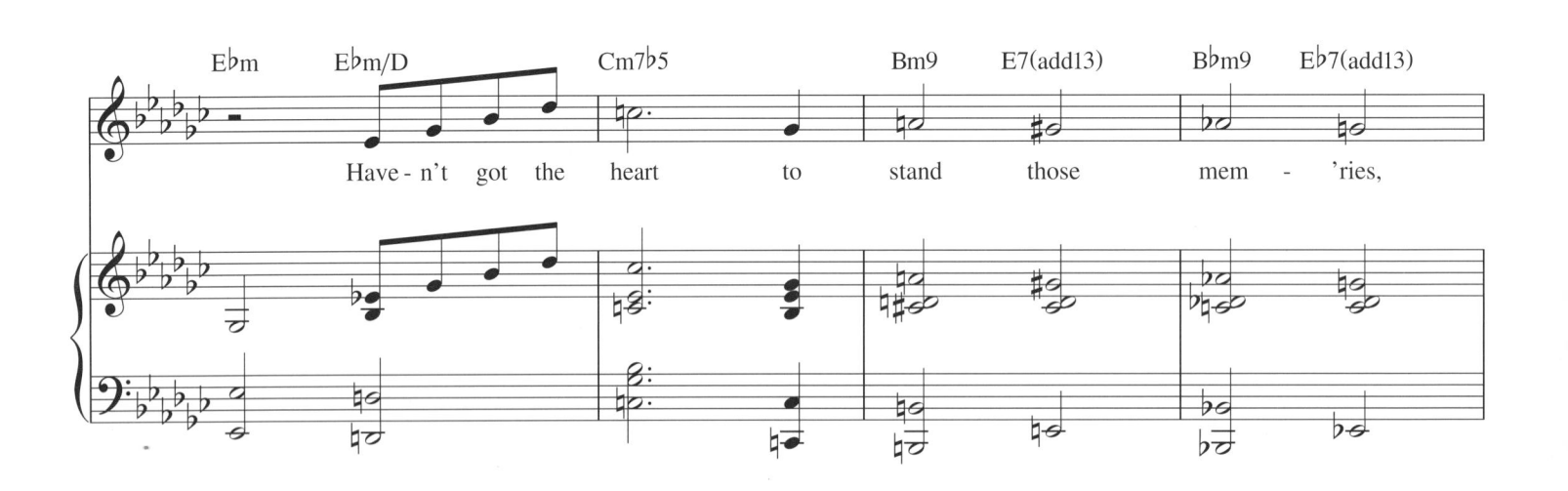

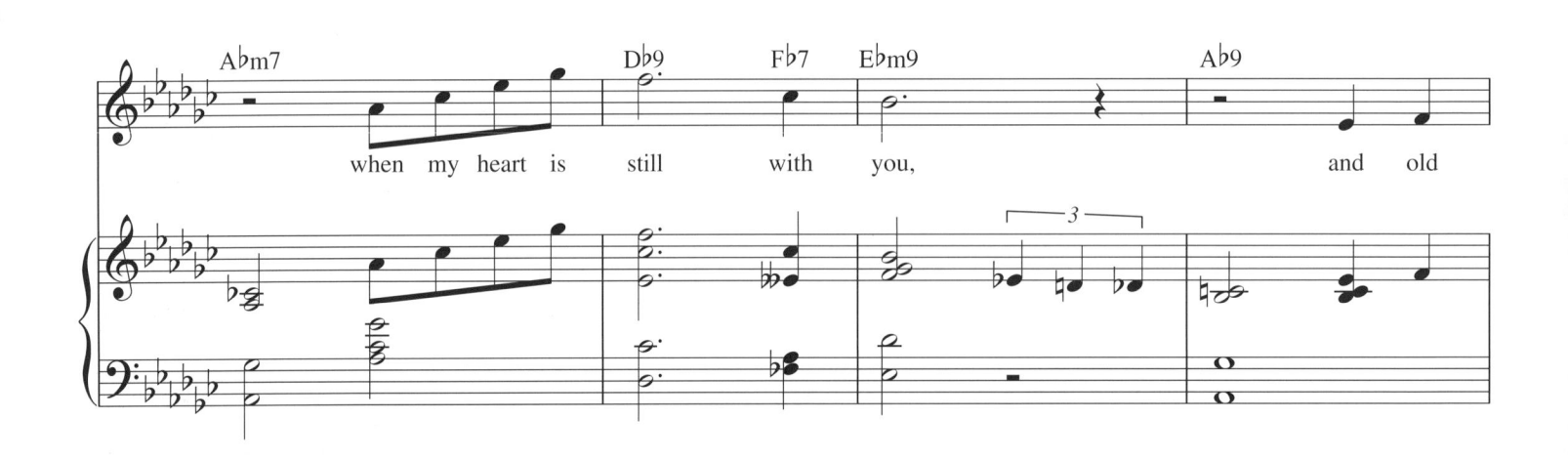

Have-n't got the heart to stand those mem-'ries,

when my heart is still with you, and old

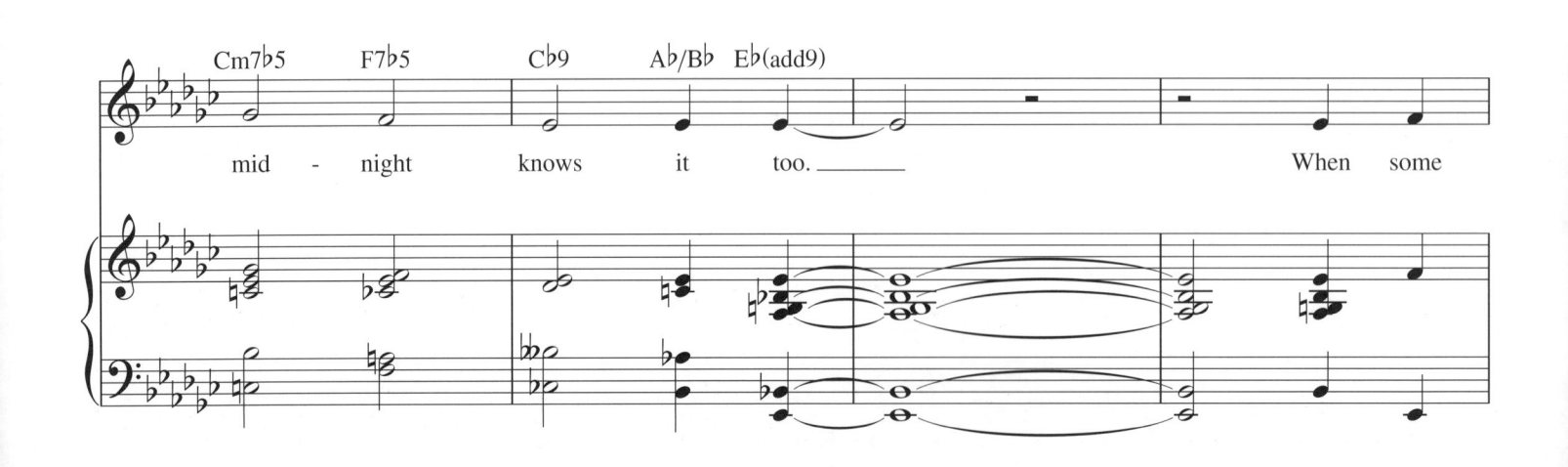

mid-night knows it too. When some

quar-rel we had ___ needs mend-ing, does it mean that our love ___ is end-ing? Dar-ling, I need you; late-ly I find ___ you're out of my arms and I'm out of my mind.

Let our love take wing some mid-night, 'round mid-night.

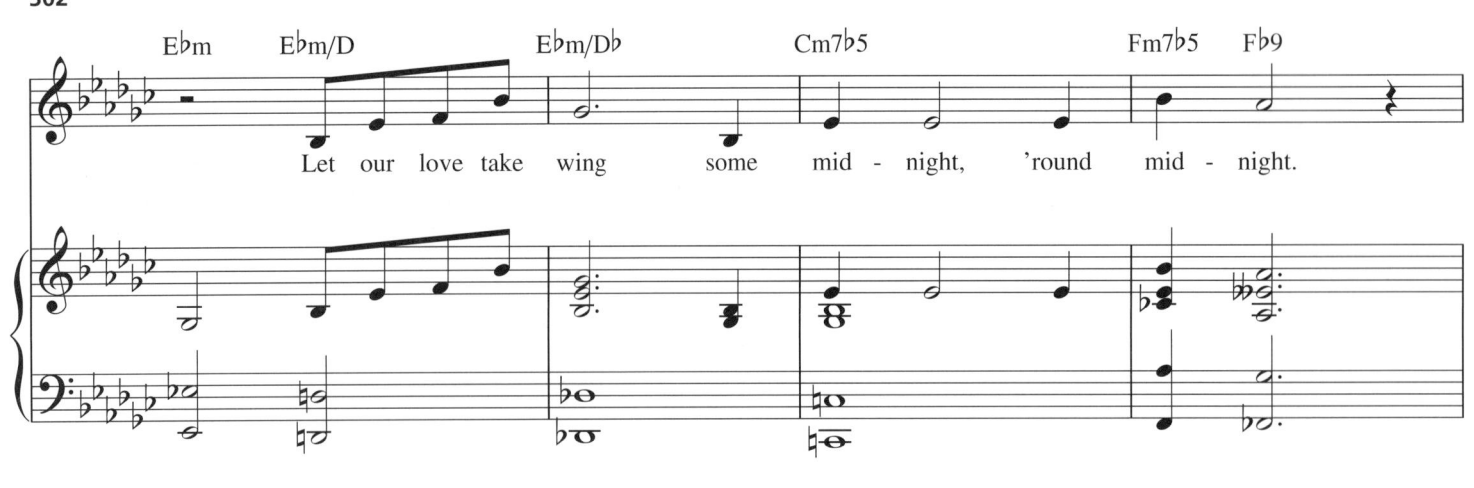

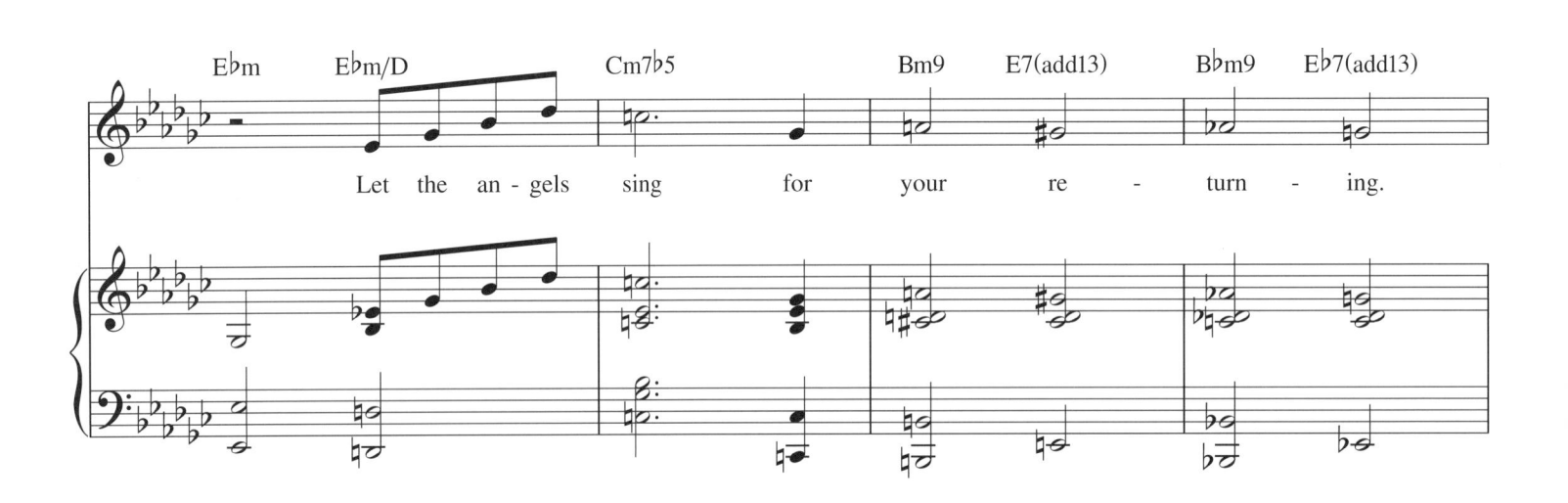

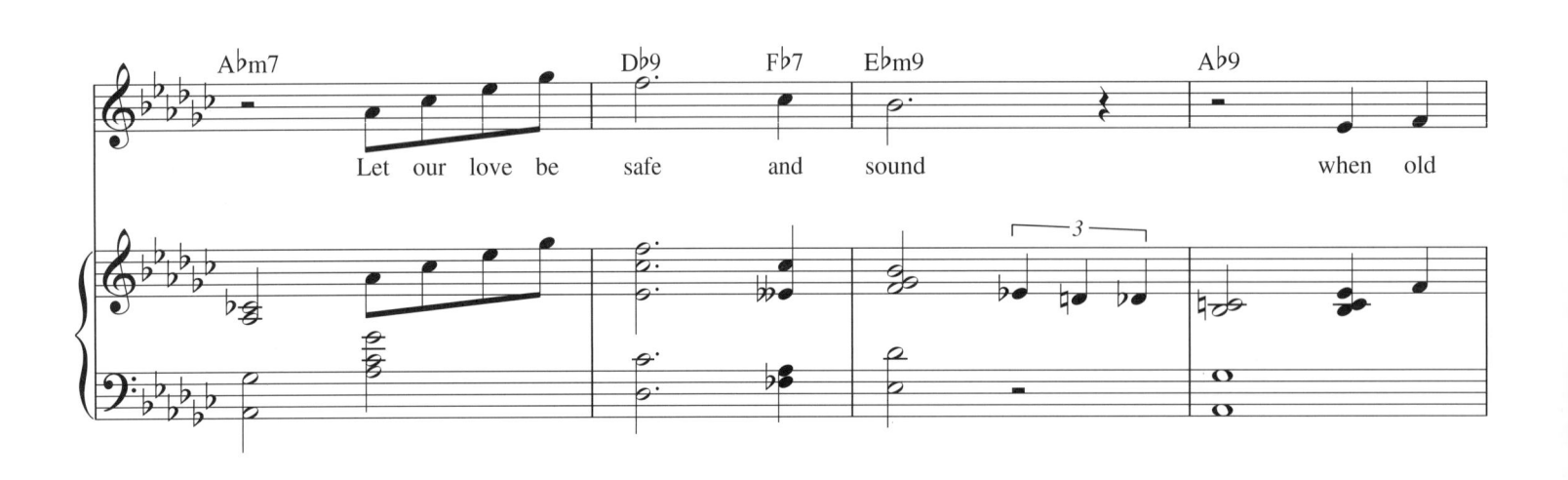

Let the an-gels sing for your re-turn-ing.

Let our love be safe and sound when old

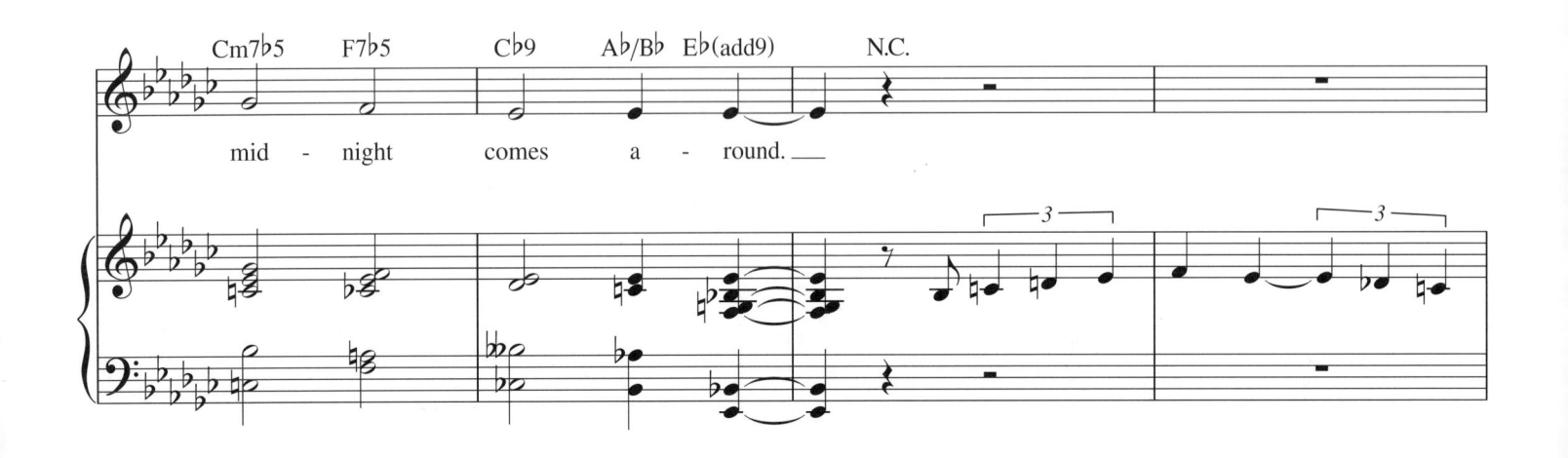

mid-night comes a-round.

Cm7♭5
C♭7
Cm7♭5
C♭7
F♯m7
B7
Am7
B7
D6/E
Fm7
B♭13♯11
E♭m7
C♯m9
F♯9
Bm9
E9
Am9
B♭7♭5
E♭6/9
rit.

'S WONDERFUL
from FUNNY FACE

Music and Lyrics by GEORGE GERSHWIN
and IRA GERSHWIN

Moderately

Life has just be-gun. Jack has found his Jill.
Don't mind tell-ing you, in my hum-ble fash,

Don't know what you've done, but I'm all a-thrill.
that you thrill me through with a ten-der pash.

How can words ex-press your di-vine ap-peal?
When you said you care, 'mag-ine my e-mosh.

© 1927 (Renewed) WB MUSIC CORP.
All Rights Reserved Used by Permission

You can nev-er guess all the love I feel.
I swore then and there per-ma-nent de-vosh.

From now on, la-dy, I in-sist
You made all oth-er boys seem blah.

for me no oth-er girls ex-ist.
Just you a-lone filled me with "ah!"

'S won-der-ful! 'S mar-vel-ous!

You should care for me! 'S awful nice! 'S paradise! 'S what I love to see!

You've made my life so My dear, it's four-leaf

glam - or - ous. _____
clo - ver time. _____ You can't blame me for feel - ing
From now on my heart's work - ing

am - or - ous. _____
o - ver - time. _____ Oh! 'S won - der - ful! _____

'S mar - vel - ous! _____ That you should care _____ for

1. me!

2. me! _____

ST. THOMAS

By SONNY ROLLINS

C6
B♭7
A7
Dm7
A♭7♯5
G7
To Coda
C6
C9/E
F6
F♯dim7
C/G
G7
C6
1
G7
2
G7
C6
Em7
A7
D7
G7♭9
C6
Em7
A7♭9

D9
G7
C6
B♭7
A7
D7
A♭7♭9
G7
C6
C9/E
F6
F♯dim7
C/G
A7
Dm7
G9
C6
Em7
A7
Dm7
G7♯5(♭9)
C6

Em7
A7
Dm7
G7
C6
B♭9
A7♯9
Dm
A♭7
Dm7/G
G7
C6
C9/E
F
F♯dim7
C/G
A7♭9
Dm7
G7
C6
D.S. al Coda
CODA
C/G
G7♭9
C6
N.C.

THE SHADOW OF YOUR SMILE
Love Theme from THE SANDPIPER

Music by JOHNNY MANDEL
Words by PAUL FRANCIS WEBSTER

Moderately, in slow 2

Rubato, in 2

One day we walked a- long the sand, One day in ear-ly spring. You held a pip-er in your hand to mend its bro-ken wing, Now I'll re-mem-ber

© 1965 METRO-GOLDWYN-MAYER INC.
Copyright Renewed by EMI Miller Catalog Inc. and MARISSA MUSIC
All Rights Controlled and Administered by EMI MILLER CATALOG INC. (Publishing) and ALFRED MUSIC (Print)
All Rights for MARISSA MUSIC Controlled and Administered by ALMO MUSIC CORP.
All Rights Reserved   Used by Permission

Dm Dm/C Bm7♭5 E7 B♭9 Am9 Am Am7 Cdim7
many - y a day and man - y a lone - ly mile. The ech - o of a
Bm7 Em7 Am7 Am7/D D7 C6 G6/9
pip - er's song the shad - ow of a smile.
Moderately, slow 4
N.C.
F♯m7 B7 F/B
The shad - ow of your smile when you are
mp
Em A9 Am7
gone Will col - or all my dreams and
R.H.

D7 A♭7♭5 G Cmaj13
3fr
3fr
light the dawn. Look in - to my
F♯m7♭5 F♯m7/B B7 B7♭9 Em Em7
4fr
eyes my love and see All the love - ly
C♯m7♭5 F♯7 C9 F♯m7/B B9
4fr
N.C.
things you are to me. Our wist-ful lit - tle
F♯m7 B7 F/B Em A9
5fr
star was far too high, A tear - drop kissed your
R.H.

Am7 D9 Cdim7 Bm7♭5 E7♭5(♭9) E7♭9
4fr
lips and so did I. Now when I re -
Am7 Cm7 F13 Bm7 F9♭5
3fr
7fr
mem - ber spring All the joy that love can bring,
Bm7/E E7♭9 A13 E♭9♭5 Am7(add4) Cm/D D7♭9
5fr
5fr
3fr
3fr
4fr
I will be re - mem - ber - ing the shad - ow of your
1
G6
N.C.
smile. The shad - ow of your
2
G6
smile.
mf
Ped.
*
Ped.
*

SHINY STOCKINGS

Words by ELLA FITZGERALD
Music by FRANK FOSTER

Moderately, with a beat

Female: Those silk shin-y stock-ings that I
Male: Those silk shin-y stock-ings that you

wear when I'm with you, ___ I wear 'cause you told ___ me that you
wear when I'm with you, ___ you wear 'cause I told ___ you that I

dig that cra-zy hue. ___ Do we think of ro-mance ___
dig that cra-zy hue. ___ When we go to a dance, ___

© 1956, 1965. Renewed. Published by Lynnstorm Publishing Co. c/o Helen Blue Musique and Larry Spier Music LLC, New York, NY
All Rights Reserved   Used by Permission

317

a - bout me, why, I nev - er knew. ___ I
a - bout me, why, I nev - er knew. ___ I

guess I'll have to find ___ a new find, a new kind, ___
guess I'll have to find ___ a new find, a new kind, ___

a guy who digs my shin - y stock - ings, too. ___
a gal who wears those shin - y stock - ings, too. ___

Those ___
Those ___

SOMEONE TO WATCH OVER ME

from OH, KAY!

Music and Lyrics by GEORGE GERSHWIN
and IRA GERSHWIN

There's a say-ing old Says that love is blind, Still we're of-ten told, "Seek and ye shall find." So I'm going to seek A cer-tain lad I've had in mind. Look-ing ev-'ry-where, Have-n't

© 1926 (Renewed) WB MUSIC CORP.
All Rights Reserved   Used by Permission

where is the shep-herd for this lost lamb?

There's a some-bod-y I'm long-ing to see. I hope that he Turns out to be Some-one who'll watch o-ver me.

I'm a lit-tle lamb who's

lost in the wood. I know I could Al - ways be good To one who'll watch o - ver me. Al - though he may not be the man some Girls think of as hand - some, To my heart he car - ries the key.

Won't you tell him please to put on some speed, Fol - low my lead,

Oh, how I need Some - one to watch o - ver

1. me.

2. me.

Spring Can Really Hang You Up the Most

Lyric by FRAN LANDESMAN
Music by TOMMY WOLF

Once I was a sentimental thing, threw my heart away each spring. Now a spring romance hasn't got a chance, promised my first dance to winter, all I've got to show's a

Copyright © 1955 by Wolf Mills, Inc., c/o Fricout Music Company, 134 Bluegrass Circle, Hendersonville, TN 37075
Copyright Renewed
Copyright © 1987 Assigned to WOLFLAND, Admin. by Fricout Music Company, 134 Bluegrass Circle, Hendersonville, TN 37075
International Copyright Secured   All Rights Reserved

splin - ter for my lit - tle fling!

Slowly

Spring this year has got me feel - ing __ like a horse that nev - er left the post;
Spring is here, there's no mis - tak - ing, __ rob - ins build - ing nests from coast to coast;

I lie in my room, __ star - ing up at the ceil - ing.
my heart tries to sing __ so they won't hear it break - ing.

Spring can real - ly hang you up the most!

Morn - ing's kiss wakes
Col - lege boys are

trees and flow-ers, ___ and to them I'd like to drink a toast; I
writ-ing son-nets, ___ in the "ten-der pas-sion" they're en-grossed; but

walk in the park ___ just to kill lone-ly hours. ___
I'm on the shelf ___ with last year's Eas-ter bon-nets.

Spring can real-ly hang you up the most! All af-ter-noon, those
Love came my way, I

birds __ twit-ter twit, I know the tune: "This is love, __ this is it!"
hoped __ it would last; we had our day, now it's all __ in the past.

Cm7
Fmaj7/C
Cm7
Fmaj7/C
3fr
3fr
Heard it be - fore and I know the score;
Spring came a - long, a sea - son of song;
F♯m7
Emaj7
Am7
D7
3
3
and I've de - cid - ed that spring is a bore!
full of sweet prom - ise, but some - thing went wrong!
Gmaj7
Fmaj7
Cmaj7
B♭maj7
Love seemed sure a - round the New Year,
Doc - tors once pre - scribed a ton - ic:
Am7/G
Dm7
G7
Em7
A7♭9
5fr
5fr
now it's A - pril, love is just a ghost.
"sul - phur and mo - las - ses" was the dose.
Spring ar -
Did - n't

F♯m7♭5
4fr
Fm7
1
Em7
Am7
D7
D7♭5/A♭
rived on time, on - ly what be - came of you, dear?
help a bit, my con -
Dm7
G7
Em7
Am7
A7
Spring can real - ly hang you up the most!
Dm7
G7
Cmaj7
B♭maj7
B♭7
Spring can real - ly hang you up the most!
2
E♭m7
6fr
A7
A♭7
4fr
Dm7
G7
di - tion must be chron - ic. Spring can real - ly hang you up the

most! All a - lone, the par-ty's o - ver, old man win-ter was a gra-cious host; but when you keep pray-ing for snow to hide the clo - ver, spring can real - ly hang you up the most!

SPRING IS HERE
from I MARRIED AN ANGEL

Words by LORENZ HART
Music by RICHARD RODGERS

are sad-ly out of tune. Life has stuck the pin in the bal-loon.

poco rit.

Refrain *(slowly, with expression)*

Spring is here! Why does-n't my heart go danc-ing? Spring is here! Why is-n't the waltz en-tranc-ing? No de-sire,

Lyrics:
No am-bi-tion leads me, May-be it's be-cause no-bod-y needs me. Spring is here! Why does-n't the breeze de-light me? Stars ap-

pear; Why doesn't the night invite me?

Maybe it's because nobody loves me. Spring is here, I

hear! hear!

SQUEEZE ME

*Words and Music by CLARENCE WILLIAMS
and THOMAS "FATS" WALLER*

Dad - dy, you've been dog - gone sweet on me, dad - dy, you the on - ly one I see; you know I need but you 'cause you my man you can love me like no one

Copyright © 1925 UNIVERSAL MUSIC CORP. and GREAT STANDARDS MUSIC PUBLISHING COMPANY
Copyright Renewed
All Rights for GREAT STANDARDS MUSIC PUBLISHING COMPANY Controlled and Administered by THE SONGWRITERS GUILD OF AMERICA
All Rights Reserved   Used by Permission

335

C7 B7♯5 C7 D7 G9 C7 F E♭maj7 D7
9fr
3fr
fore. Your pa - pa cu - pid is stand - ing close by.
Now, dad - dy,
Dad - dy,
G9 C7 F7 F9 F7 Bdim B♭m6 F♯dim/A G♯dim Edim/G
9fr
6fr
3fr
3fr
don't let sweet ba - by
don't let sweet ma - ma
cry.
Pick me up
F7 E7 E♭7 D7
1
G9 G9/D G9/D♭ C7 C7♯5 F
9fr
9fr
9fr
8fr
on your knee.
I just git so, you know, when you squeeze me. Now, dad - dy,
2
G9 C6 C7♯5 F7
9fr
8fr
I just git so, you know, Dad - dy, when you squeeze me.
rall.

STAR EYES

Words by DON RAYE
Music by GENE DePAUL

Bossa Nova

338

G6/9
Gm7♭5
C13
C7♯5
F6/9
E♭9
D9
cresc.
Gm11/C
3
ff
Fdim(maj7)
F6
E♭9
D9
Gm11
mp
3
8va
G♭
mf
3
F6/9
f
Fmaj9

Stars Fell on Alabama

Words by MITCHELL PARISH
Music by FRANK PERKINS

Moon-light and mag-no-lia, star-light in your hair,

© 1934 (Renewed) EMI MILLS MUSIC INC.
All Rights Administered by EMI MILLS MUSIC INC. (Publishing) and ALFRED MUSIC (Print)
All Rights Reserved Used by Permission

all the world a dream come true. Did it really happen, was I really there, was I really there with you? We lived our little drama, we kissed in a field of white, and stars fell on Alabama last night. I can't forget the glamour, your eyes held a tender light, and stars fell on Alabama last night.

I never planned in my imagination a situ-

a - tion so heav - en - ly. A fair - y land where no one else could en - ter, and in the cen - ter just you and me, dear. My heart beat like a ham - mer, my arms wound a - round you tight, and stars fell on Al - a - bam - a last night. night.

STREET OF DREAMS

By SAM M. LEWIS and VICTOR YOUNG

new dreams for old. I know where they're bought, I know where they're sold.
ringing with cheer, 'cause yesterday's gone, to-mor-row is near.

Mid - night, _____ you've got to get there at mid - night. _____
Mid - night, _____ the heart is light - er at mid - night. _____

—— And you'll be met there by oth - ers like you, broth - ers as blue,
—— Things will be bright - er the mo - ment you find more of your kind

E♭m
Fm7♭5
B♭7
B♭7♯5
B♭7
B♭7♭9
smil-ing on the street of dreams.
smil-ing on the street of dreams.
Love laughs at a king, kings don't mean a
E♭maj7
E♭6
Edim7
B♭7
thing, on the street of dreams.
Dreams bro - ken in
B♭7♭9
E♭9
E♭7
two can be made like new on the street of dreams.

Gold, silver and gold, all you can hold is in the moon-beams. Poor, no one is poor, long as love is sure on the street of dreams. dreams.

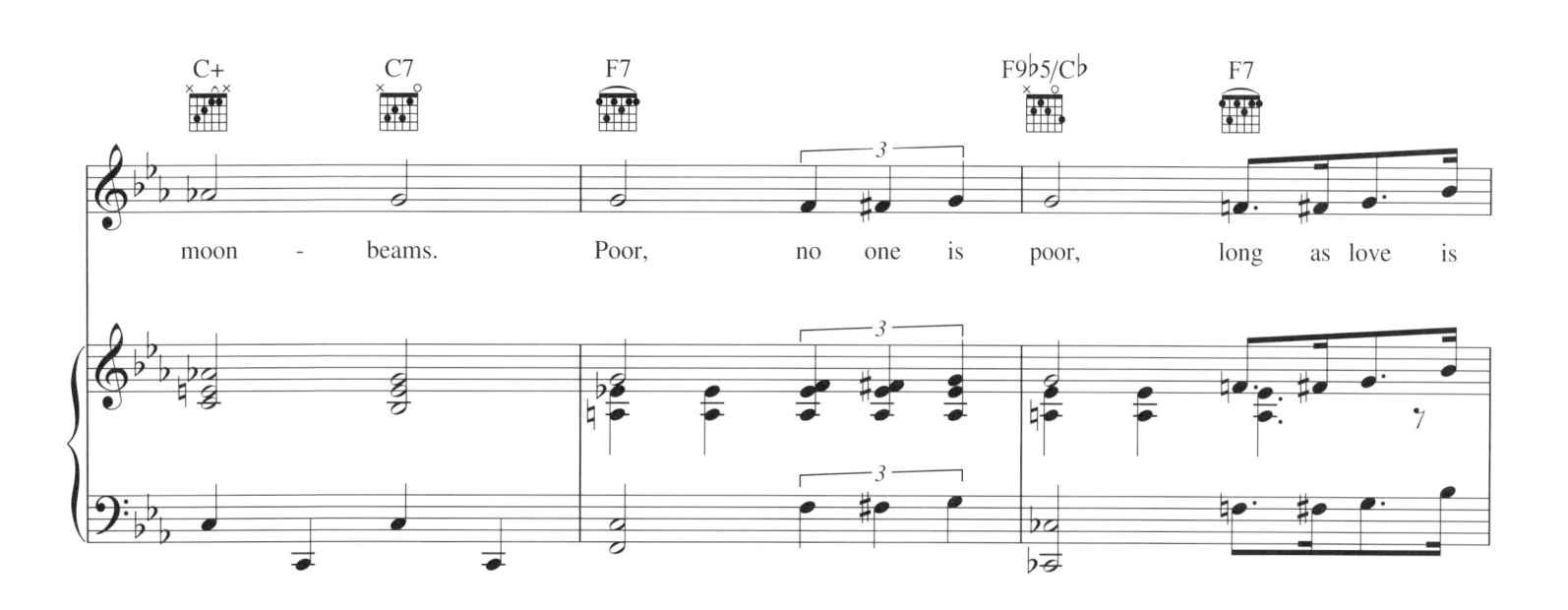

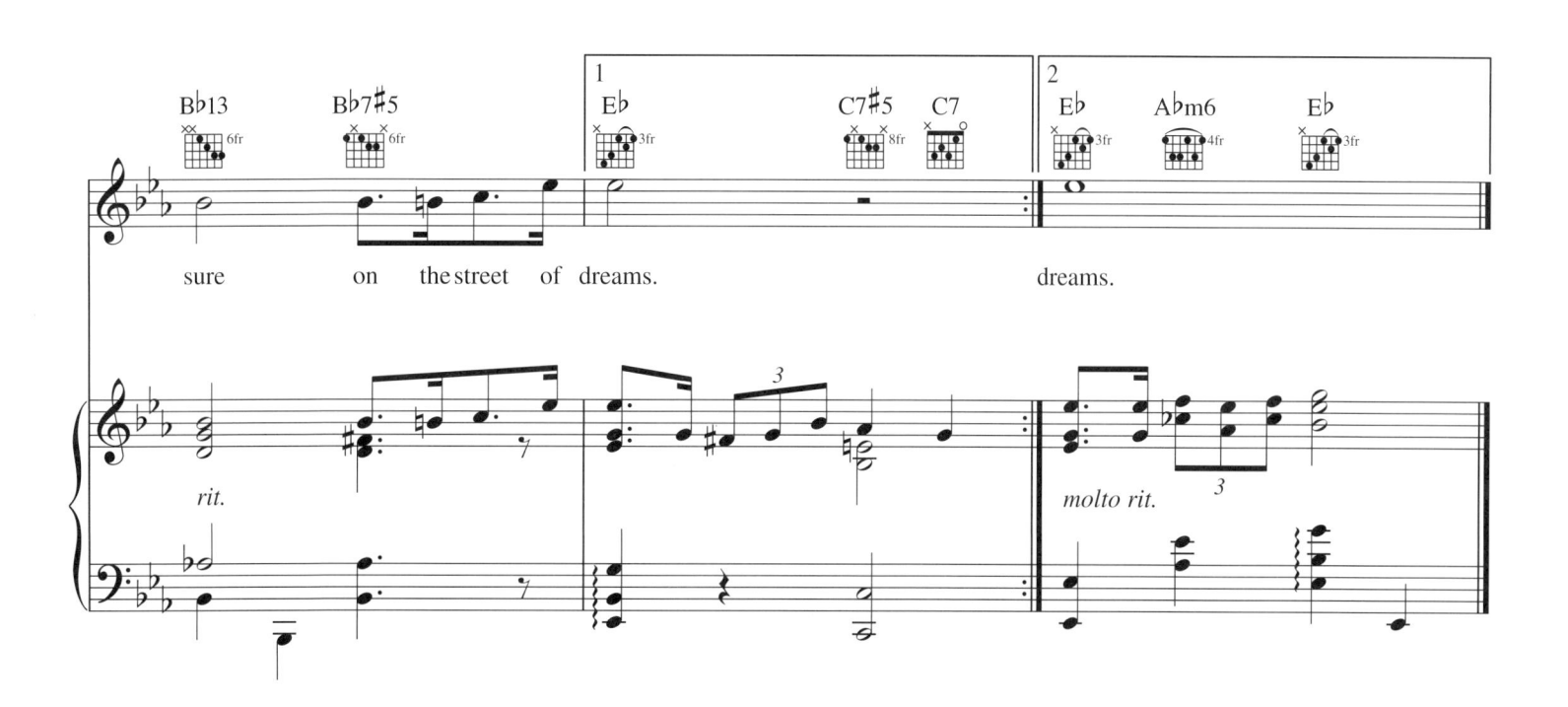

SUMMERTIME
from PORGY AND BESS®

Music and Lyrics by GEORGE GERSHWIN,
DU BOSE and DOROTHY HEYWARD
and IRA GERSHWIN

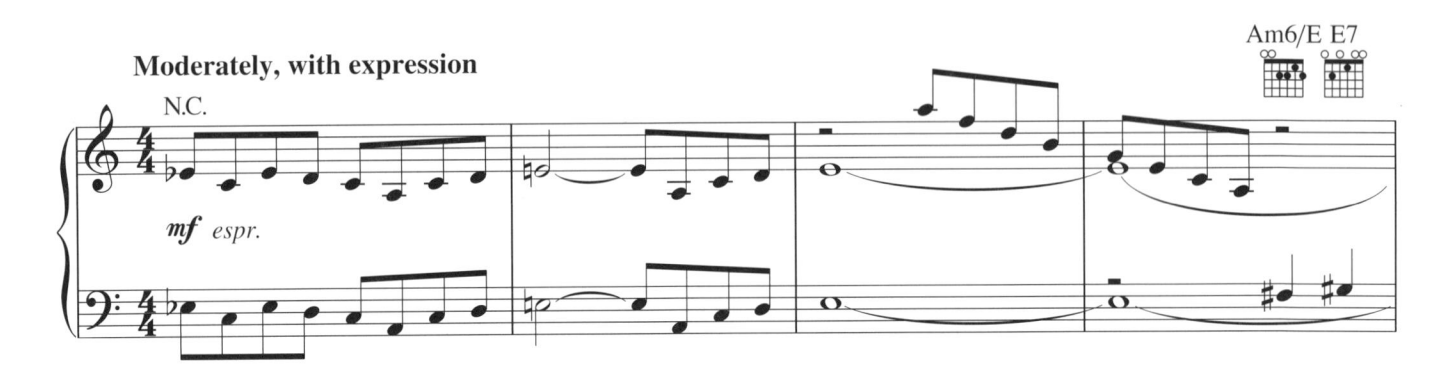

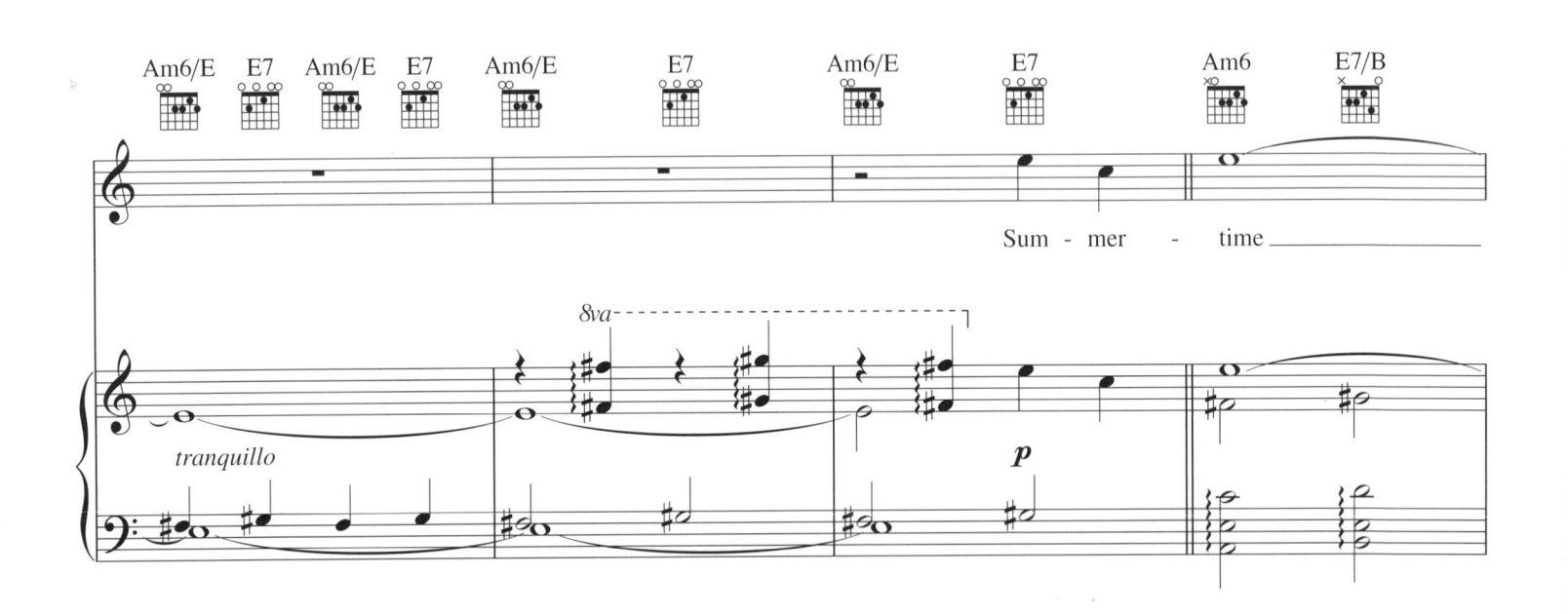

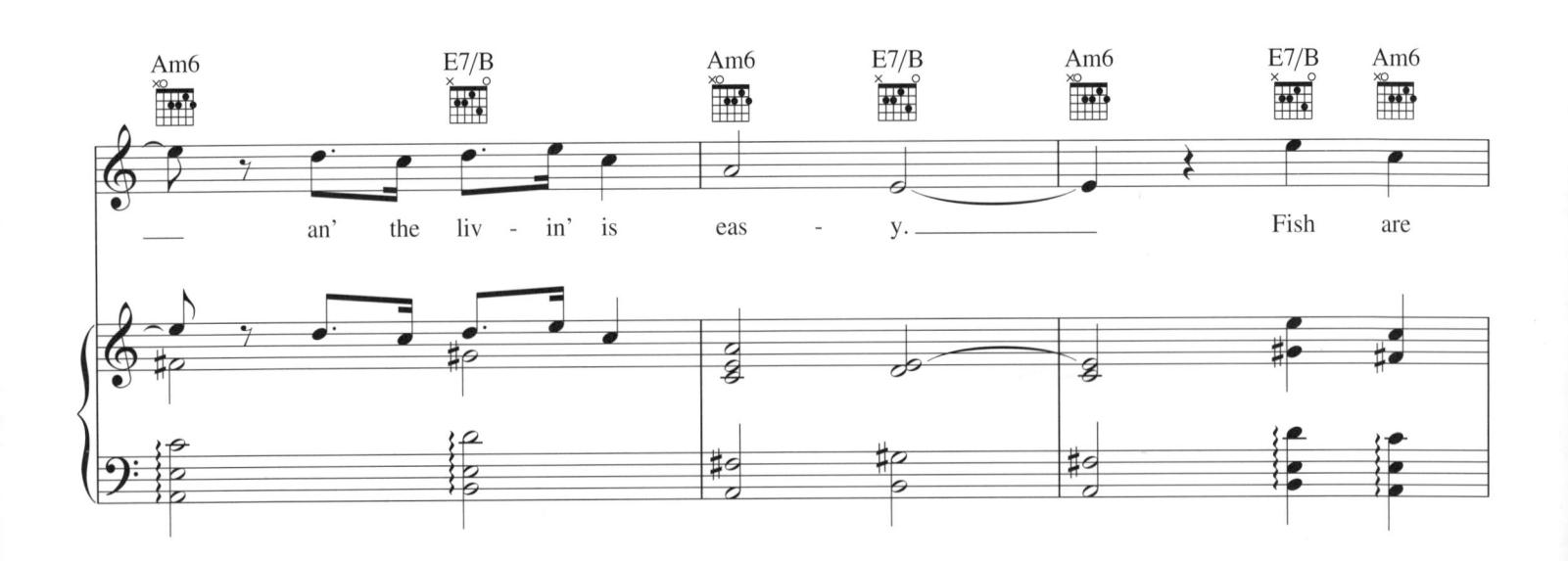

© 1935 (Renewed) GEORGE GERSHWIN MUSIC, IRA GERSHWIN MUSIC and DU BOSE AND DOROTHY HEYWARD MEMORIAL FUND
All Rights Administered by WB MUSIC CORP.
All Rights Reserved   Used by Permission

jump-in' _____ an' the cot-ton is high. _____

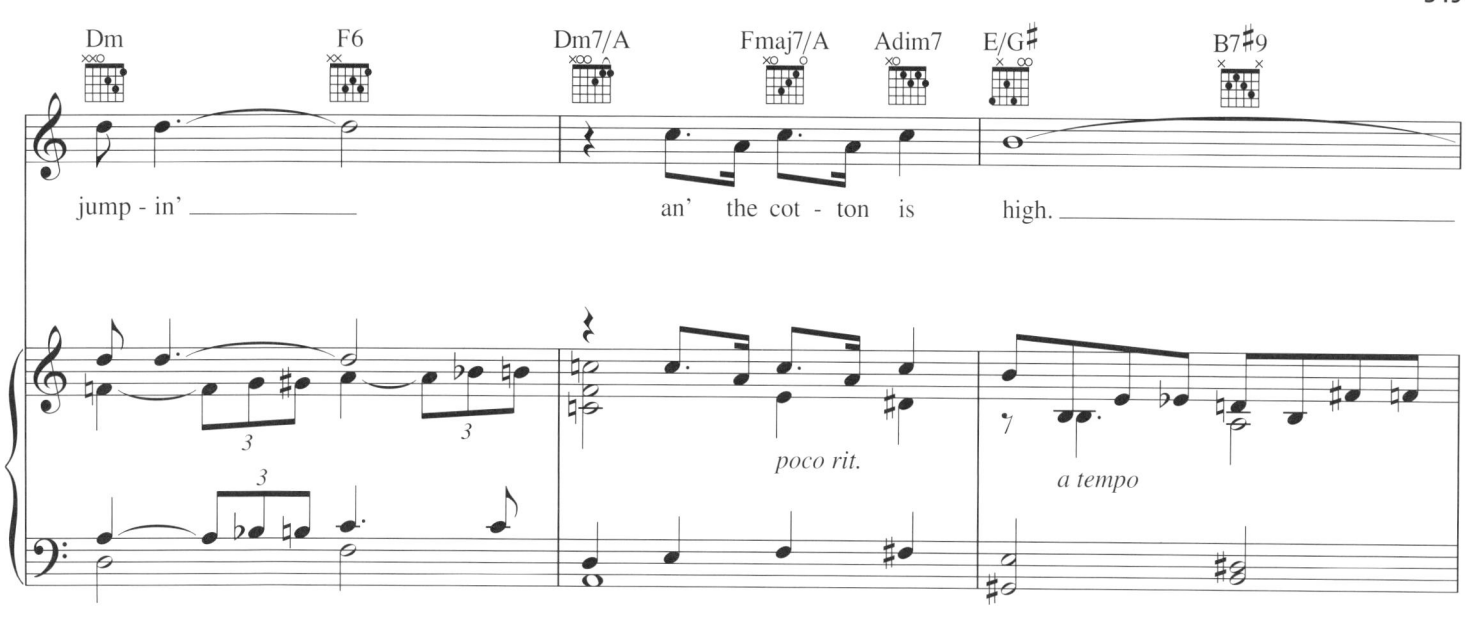

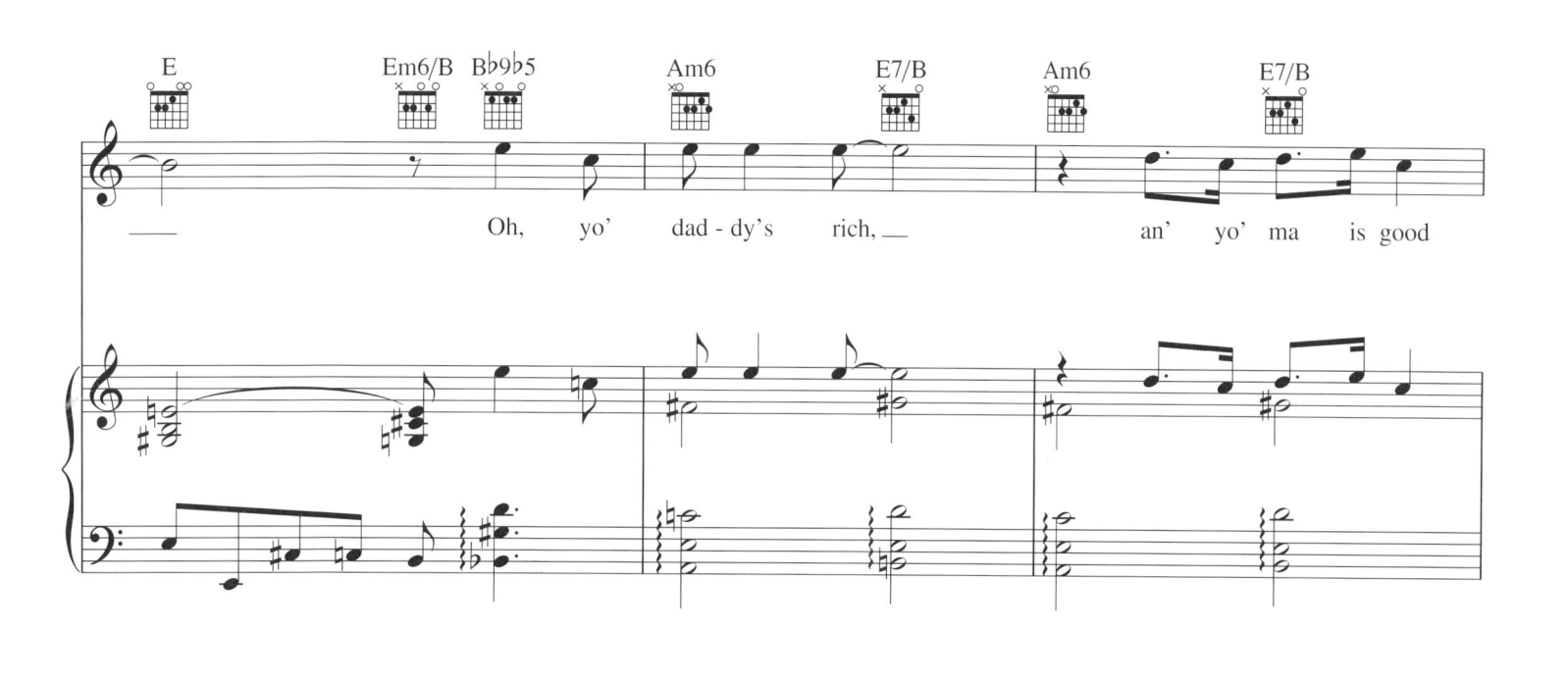

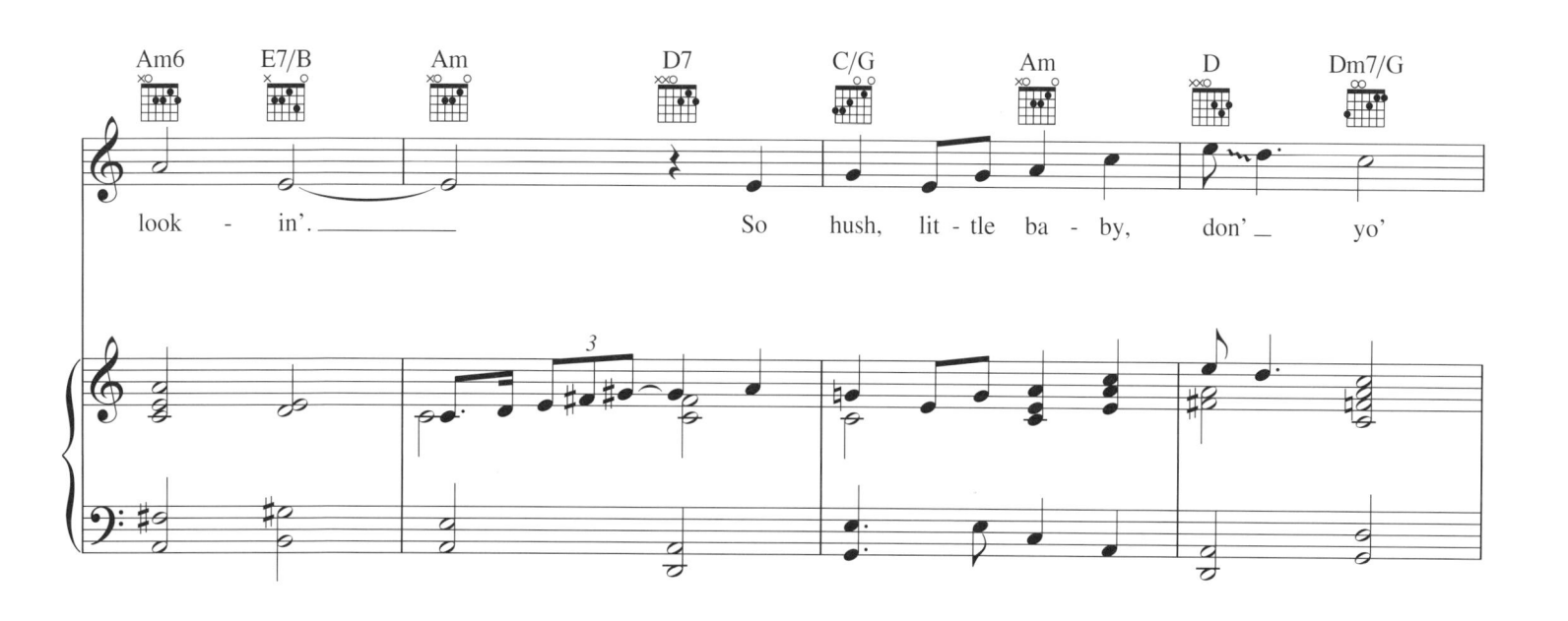

Oh, yo' dad-dy's rich, ____ an' yo' ma is good

look-in'. _____ So hush, lit-tle ba-by, don' _ yo'

cry. _____ One of these morn-in's you goin' to rise __ up sing - in'. _____ Then you'll spread yo' wings __ an' you'll take __ the sky. _____

But till that mornin' there's a nothin' can harm you, with Daddy an' Mammy standin' by.

morendo

pp

SWEET GEORGIA BROWN

Words and Music by BEN BERNIE,
MACEO PINKARD and KENNETH CASEY

She just got here yes-ter-day, ___ *things are hot here now they say,* ___ *there's* ___ *a big change in*
Brown-skin gals you'll get the blues, ___ *brown-skin pals you'll sure-ly lose,* ___ *and* ___ *there's but one ex-*

© 1925 (Renewed) WB MUSIC CORP.
All Rights Reserved Used by Permission

Em
B7
town.
cuse.
Gals are jeal - ous, there's no doubt,
Now I've told you who she was
Em
B7
A7
still the fel - lows rave a - bout.
and I've told you what she does.
Sweet,
Hand
D7
Sweet Geor - gia Brown.
this gal her dues.
And
This
B7
ev - er since she came the col - ored folks all claim:
col - ered maid - en's prayer is an - swered an - y - where.
Say,

E7
no gal made has got a shade on Sweet Georgia Brown.
No gal made

A7
Two left feet, but oh so neat, has Sweet Georgia Brown.

D7   **D7#5**
They all sigh and wan-na die for Sweet Georgia Brown. I'll tell you just

G   **D7**   **D7#5**   **G**   **Em7**   **B7**

(spoken ad lib.)
why, you know I don't lie, not much!

E7
It's been said she knocks 'em dead when she lands in town.
All those tips the por - ter slips to Sweet Geor-gia Brown.
A7
B7
Em
Since she came, why it's a shame how she cools 'em down. Fel - lers
They buy clothes at fash-ion shows with one dol - lar down. Oh boy,
B7
Em
B7
G
she can't get are fel - lers she ain't met. Geor - gia claimed her,
tip your hats; oh joy, she's the "cat's." Who's that, mis - ter?
B7♭5
E7
A7
D7
1
G
B7
2
G
D7
G
Geor - gia named her Sweet Geor-gia Brown.
'Tain't her sis - ter, Sweet Geor-gia Brown.

SWEET LORRAINE

Words by MITCHELL PARISH
Music by CLIFF BURWELL

Moderately

Ev-'ry-thing is set, _____ skies are blue. Can't be-lieve it yet, _____ but it's true.
Oh, the sun is bright, _____ life seems good; For she said last night _____ that she would,

© 1928 (Renewed) EMI Mills Music Inc.
All Rights Administered by EMI MILLS MUSIC INC. (Publishing) and ALFRED MUSIC (Print)
All Rights Reserved Used by Permission

I'll give you just one guess. My sweet Lor-raine said, "Yes."
there in the gar-den lane. I mean my sweet Lor-raine.

Wait-ing for the time, soon to be, when the bells will chime mer-ri-ly.
When that day in June rolls a-round, on our hon-ey-moon we'll be bound.

Gee, but I feel proud, want to shout right out loud:
Can't wait 'til the day when I'll take her a-way: I've

Slowly

just found joy, I'm as hap-py as a ba-by boy with an-oth-er brand-new choo-choo toy, _____ when I'm with my sweet Lor - raine. _____ A

pair of eyes _____ that are blu - er than the sum - mer skies _____ when you see them you will

re - a - lize _____ why I love my sweet Lor - raine. (I'm so hap - py)

When it's rain-ing I don't miss the sun, for it's in my sweet-ie's smile, _____ just to think that I'm the luck-y one who will lead her down the aisle. Each night I pray that no-bod-y steals her heart a-way. Just can't wait un-til that hap-py day, when I mar-ry sweet Lor-raine. I've raine.

TAKING A CHANCE ON LOVE

Words by JOHN LA TOUCHE and TED FETTER
Music by VERNON DUKE

Moderately

I thought love's game was over, Lady Luck had gone a-way. I laid my cards on the table un-a-ble to play then I heard good for-tune say, "They're

© 1940 (Renewed) EMI Miller Catalog Inc. and TAKING A CHANCE ON LOVE MUSIC CO. c/o THE SONGWRITERS GUILD OF AMERICA
All Rights Reserved   Used by Permission

dealing you a new hand today!" Oh

Here I
Here I
Here I

go again I hear those trumpets blow again all a-
come again I'm gonna make things hum again act-ing
slip again about to take that tip again got my

glow again taking a chance on love. Here I
dumb again taking a chance on love. Here I
grip again taking a chance on love. Now I

slide a-gain___ a-bout to take that ride a-gain___ star-ry-
stand a-gain___ a-bout to beat the band a-gain___ feel-ing
prove a-gain___ that I can make life move a-gain___ in the

eyed a-gain___ tak-ing a chance on love. I thought that cards___ were a
grand a-gain___ tak-ing a chance on love. I nev-er dreamed___ in my
groove a-gain___ tak-ing a chance on love. I walk a-round___ with a

frame-up,___ I nev-er___ would try. But now I'm tak-ing the
slum-bers,___ and bets were___ ta-boo. But now I'm play-ing the
horse-shoe,___ in clo-ver___ I lie. And Broth-er Rab-bit, of

game up___ and the ace of hearts is high. Things are
num - bers___ on a lit - tle dream for two. Wad - ing
course, you___ bet - ter kiss your foot good - bye. On the

mend - ing now___ I see a rain - bow blend - ing now___ we'll have our hap - py
is a - gain___ I'm lead - in' with my chin a - gain___ I'm start - in' out to
ball a - gain___ I'm rid - in' for a fall a - gain___ I'm gon - na give my

end - ing now___ tak - ing a chance on love.
win a - gain___ tak - ing a chance on love.
all a - gain___ tak - ing a chance on love.

THAT'S ALL

*Words and Music by BOB HAYMES
and ALAN E. BRANDT*

Slowly, with expression

I can only give you love that lasts forever, ___ and the promise to be near each time you call; and the

Gm7 C9 Cm7 C♯dim7 Dm Dm7 G7
only heart I own, for you and you alone. That's all, that's
F♯7♭5 F7 B♭ F7 B♭maj7 F7
all. I can only give you country walks in springtime, and a
Dm7 G9 Cm7 F7
hand to hold when leaves begin to fall, and a
Gm7 C9 Cm7 C♯dim7
love whose burning light will warm the winter night. That's

all, that's all. There are those, I am sure, who have told you they would give you the world for a toy. All I have are these arms to en-fold you and a love time can nev-er de-stroy. If you're won-d'ring what I'm ask-ing in re-turn, dear, you'll be glad to know that my demands are small: say it's me that you'll adore, for now and evermore. That's all, that's all.

I can all.

THERE IS NO GREATER LOVE

Words by MARTY SYMES
Music by ISHAM JONES

Copyright © 1936 (Renewed) by Music Sales Corporation (ASCAP) and Bantam Music Publishing Co.
All Rights for Bantam Music Publishing Co. Administered by WB Music Corp.
International Copyright Secured   All Rights Reserved
Reprinted by Permission

moon-beams, a-way up in the blue, but there never was a love like mine for you. There is no greater love than what I feel for you, no greater love no heart so true.

Lyrics:

There is no great-er thrill than what you bring to me, no sweet-er song than what you sing to me. You're the sweet-est thing I have ev-er known,

E7
Am
D7
D7♭5
and to think that you are mine a - lone!
3
G7
C
F
There is no great - er love in all the world, it's
E+
E7
A7
D7
G7
true, no great - er love than what I feel for
1 C
Am7/E
A♭7/E♭
G7
2 C
Fm
C
you. There is no you.
3
molto rit.

They Can't Take That Away From Me

from SHALL WE DANCE

Music and Lyrics by GEORGE GERSHWIN
and IRA GERSHWIN

With movement

Our ro-mance won't end on a sor-row-ful note, though by to-mor-row you're gone; the song is end-ed, but as the song-writ-er wrote, the

© 1936 (Renewed) GEORGE GERSHWIN MUSIC and IRA GERSHWIN MUSIC
All Rights Administered by WB MUSIC CORP.
All Rights Reserved Used by Permission

C6 D7 G6 C6 D7 Gmaj7 G6 G
mel - o - dy lin - gers on. They may take you from me, I'll
C6 D7 Gm A♭ C+ Edim Fm B♭ Edim
miss your fond ca - ress. But though they take you from me, I'll still pos -
F7 B7♭5 B♭7 A♭/B♭ E♭ Fm7/B♭ E♭/G G♭dim
sess: the way you wear your hat, the way you sip your tea,
Fm7 B♭7 Fm7 A♭/B♭ E♭ B♭7♯5 E♭9 D7♭5 B♭m6
the mem-'ry of all that, no, no, they

can't take that a-way from me! The way your smile just beams, the way you sing off key, the way you haunt my dreams, no, no, they can't take that a-way from me! We may nev-er, nev-er meet a-gain on the bump-y road to love, still I'll al-ways, al-ways keep the mem-'ry of: the way you hold your knife, _ the way we danced till three, _ the way you've changed my life. _ No, no! They can't take that a-way from me! _ No! They can't take that a-way from me! The way you wear your hat _ me! _

WALTZ FOR DEBBY

Lyric by GENE LEES
Music by BILL EVANS

Moderately, in one

In her own sweet world, populated by dolls and clowns and a prince and a big purple bear,

TRO - © 1964 (Renewed), 1965 (Renewed), 1966 (Renewed) Folkways Music Publishers, Inc., New York, NY
International Copyright Secured
All Rights Reserved Including Public Performance For Profit
Used by Permission

377

mu - sic, songs that are spun of gold some - where in her own lit - tle head. One day all too soon, she'll grow up and she'll leave her dolls and her prince and her sil - ly old

Gm7 C7♭5 C7 Am7 D7♯5 Gm7
7fr
bear. When she goes, they will cry
E♭11 E♭7 A♭maj7 A♭6 G7♯5 Cm Cm7
6fr 3fr 3fr 3fr
as they whis - per good - bye.
F7 Adim E♭6/B♭ Edim7/B♭ Fm7/B♭
5fr
They will miss her, I fear; but then, so
B♭9 B♭7♭9 E♭ E♭+ E♭6
3fr
will I.

Watch What Happens
from THE UMBRELLAS OF CHERBOURG

Music by MICHEL LEGRAND
Original French Text by JACQUES DEMY
English Lyrics by NORMAN GIMBEL

Lyrics:
Let some-one start be-liev-ing in you,
Let him hold out his hand,
Let him touch you and watch what hap-pens.
One some-one who can look in your eyes

Copyright © 1964 PRODUCTIONS MICHEL LEGRAND and PRODUCTIONS FRANCIS LEMARQUE
Copyright © 1965 UNIVERSAL - SONGS OF POLYGRAM INTERNATIONAL, INC. and JONWARE MUSIC CORP.
Copyright Renewed; English words Renewed 1993 by NORMAN GIMBEL and Assigned to WORDS WEST LLC (P.O. Box 15187, Beverly Hills, CA 90209 USA)
All Rights Reserved   Used by Permission

and see in-to your heart, Let him find you and watch what hap-pens. Cold. No, I won't be-lieve your heart is cold, May-be just a-fraid to be bro-ken a-gain. Let some-one with a deep love to give,

Give that deep love to you ____ and what mag-ic you'll see: Let some-one give his heart, Some-one who cares like me. ____

me. ____

WHISPER NOT

By BENNY GOLSON

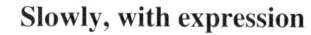

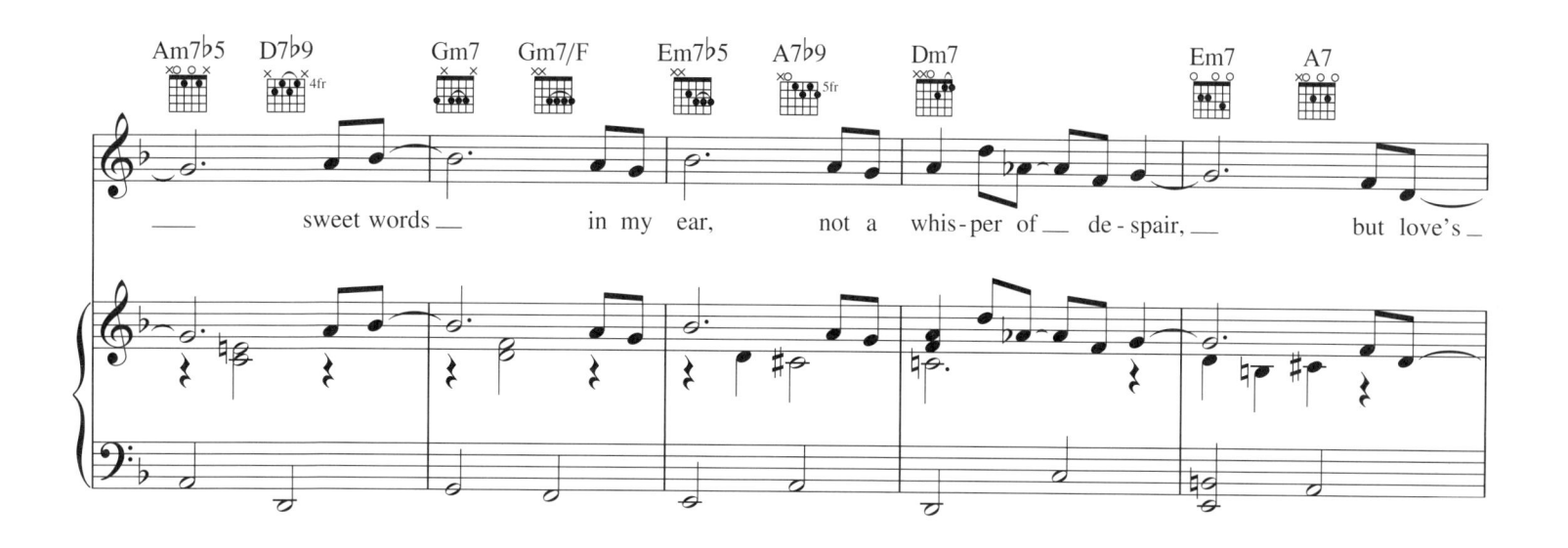

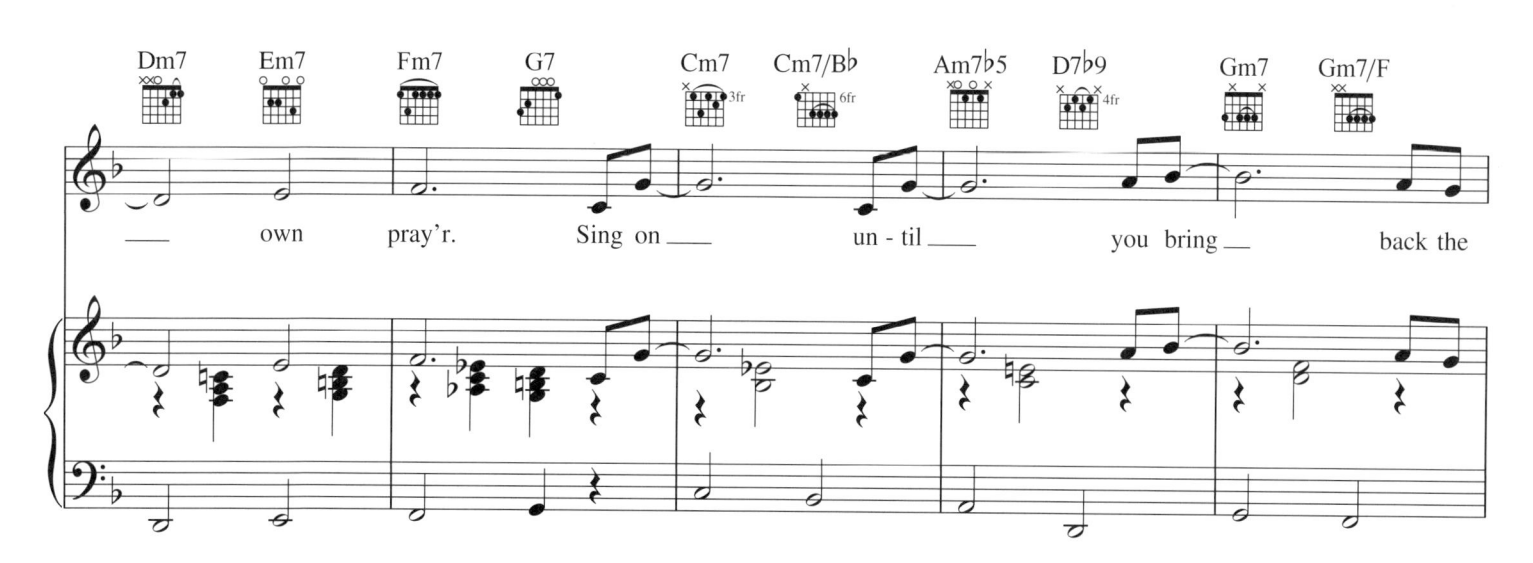

Slowly, with expression

Sing low, sing clear sweet words in my ear, not a whis-per of de-spair, but love's own pray'r. Sing on un-til you bring back the

Copyright © 1956 (Renewed 1984) IBBOB MUSIC, INC. d/b/a TIME STEP MUSIC (ASCAP)
International Copyright Secured All Rights Reserved

thrill of a sen-ti-men-tal tune____ that died____ too soon. Our har-mo-ny was lost,____ but you for-gave;_____ I for-got.____ Whis-per not of quar-rels past; you know we've had our last! So now____ we'll be____ on key____ con-stant-

ly. Love will whis-per on __ e - ter - nal - ly. __

Why did we lis-ten when they said it would-n't last? Gos-sip-ing voic-es made us
whis-pers of trou-ble are an ech-o of the past. All it-'ll take to lose my

break up, but you know we still can make up if we for-get 'em all and an-swer
gloom is just a whis-per not of ru-mors but of your love for me. That's how it's

1.
Cu-pid's call. It's the truth:__

2.
got to be! __

WAVE

Words and Music by
ANTONIO CARLOS JOBIM

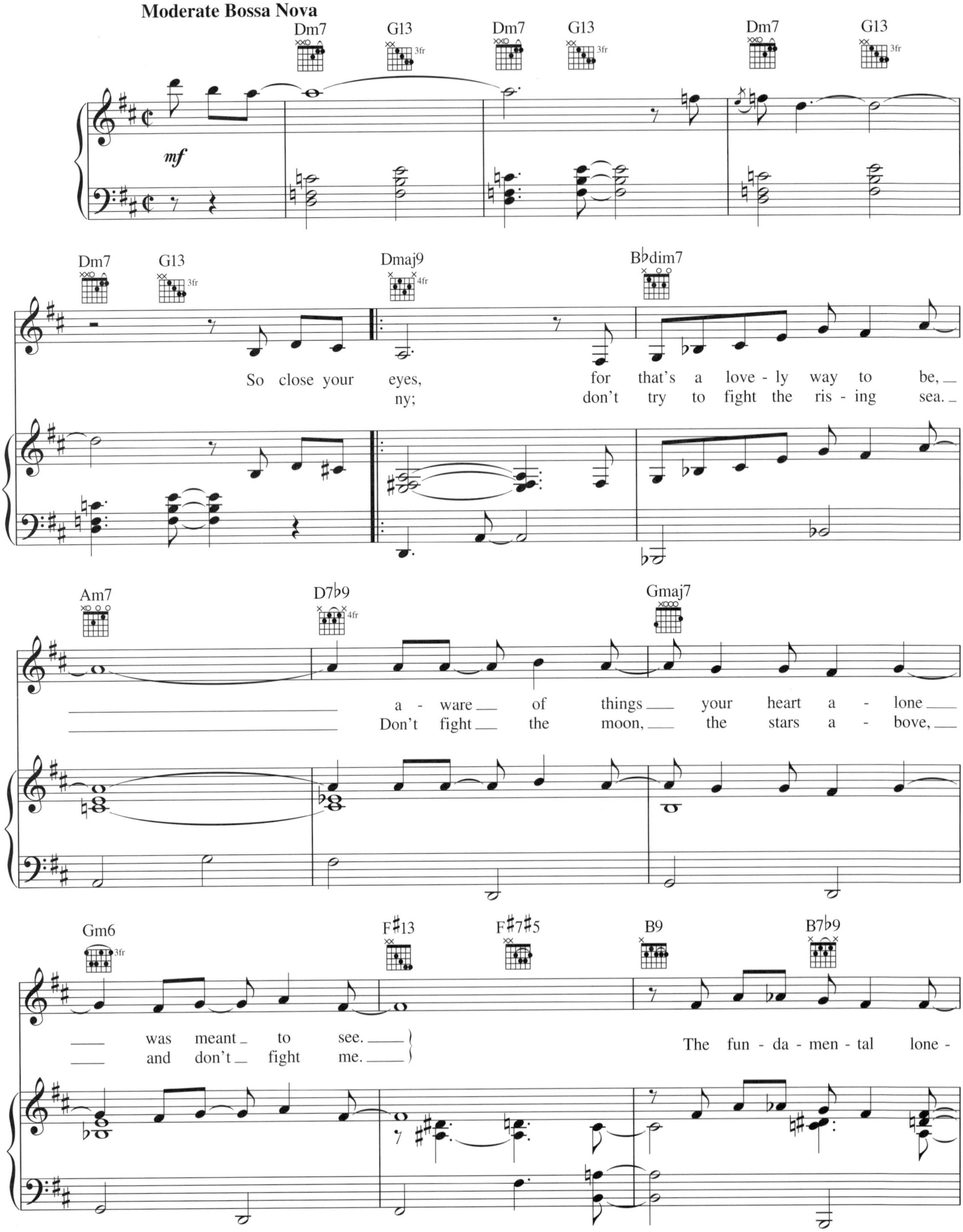

- li - ness goes__ when - ev - er two can dream a dream to - geth - er.__

You can't de - - er.__

When I saw you first, the time was half past three.__

When__ your eyes met mine, it was eter-ni-ty. _____ By now we know the wave is on its way to be. _____ Just catch __ the wave; __ don't be a-fraid _____ of lov-ing me. _____ The fun-da-men-tal lone - li-ness goes __ when-ev - er two can dream a dream to-geth-

Portuguese Lyrics

Vou te contar, os olhos já não podem ver,
Coisas que só o coração pode entender.
Fundamental é mesmo o amor,
É impossível ser feliz sozinho.

O resto é mar, é tudo que não sei contar.
São coisas lindas, que eu tenho pra te dar.
Vem de mansinho abrisa e mediz,
É impossível ser feliz sozinho.

Da primeira vez era a cidade,
Da segunda o cais e a eternidade.

Agora eu já sei, da onda que se ergueu no mar,
E das estrelas que esquecemos de contar.
O amor se deixa surpreender,
Enquanto a noite vem nos envolver.

WHAT IS THIS THING CALLED LOVE?
from WAKE UP AND DREAM

Words and Music by
COLE PORTER

Moderately

I was a hum-drum per-son, lead-ing a life a-part, when
You gave me days of sun-shine, you gave me nights of cheer, you

love flew in through my win-dow wide, and quick-ened my hum-drum heart.
made my life an en-chant-ed dream, till some-bod-y else came near.

Love flew in through my win-dow, I was so hap-py then. But
Some-bod-y else came near you, I felt the win-ter's chill. And

© 1929 (Renewed) WB MUSIC CORP.
All Rights Reserved Used by Permission

C7/E
F7
Dm7♭5
Dm7♭5/A♭
G7♯5
af - ter love had stayed a lit - tle while, love flew out a -
now I sit and won - der night and day why I love you
C
Dm7
G13
C
gain.
still?
What
Slowly
C7
Fm6
is this thing called love?
G7
G7♯5
This fun - ny thing called

love? Just who can solve ____ its myster-y? Why should it make ____ a fool of me? I saw you there ____ one wonderful day. You took my heart ____

Lyrics:
and threw it a - way. That's why I ask the Lawd in heav - en a - bove, what is this thing called love? What love?

WHEN YOUR LOVER HAS GONE

Words and Music by
E.A. SWAN

For ag - es and ag - es the po - ets and sag - es of love, won - drous love, al - ways sing. But ask an - y lov - er and you'll soon dis-

What good is the schem - ing, the plan - ning, and the dream - ing of that love comes with each new love af - fair? The love that you cher - ish so of - ten may

© 1931 (Renewed) WB MUSIC CORP.
All Rights Reserved   Used by Permission

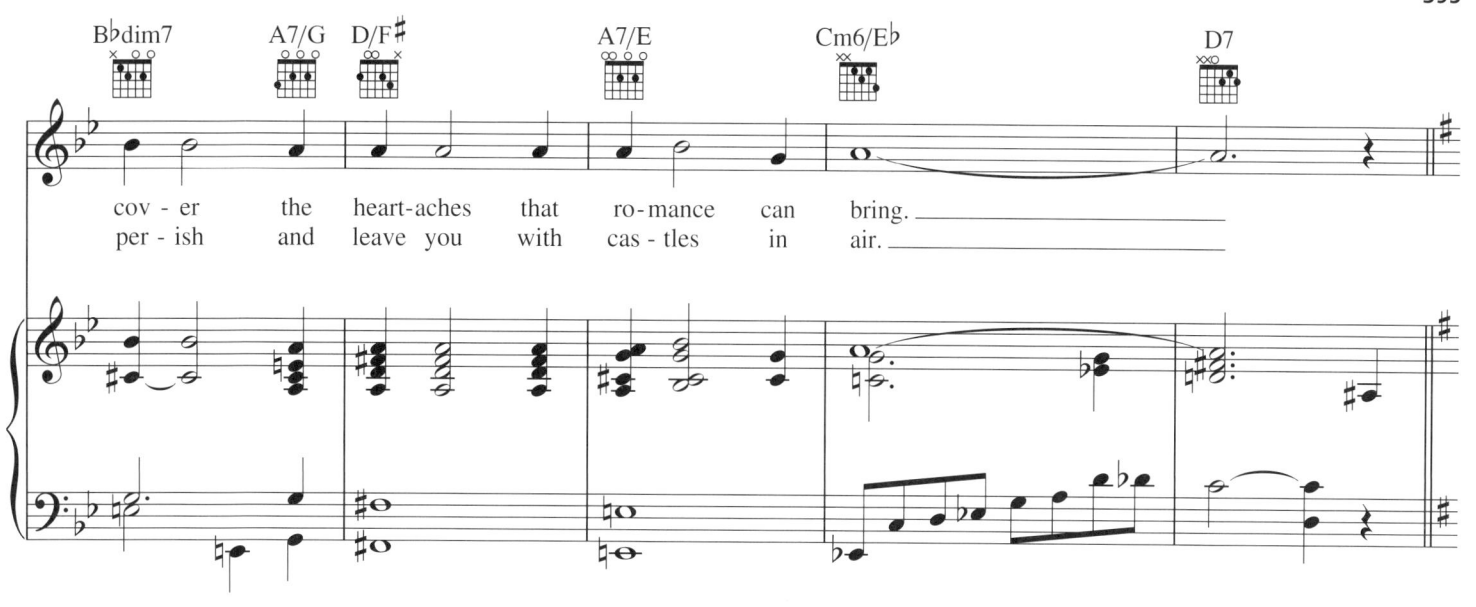

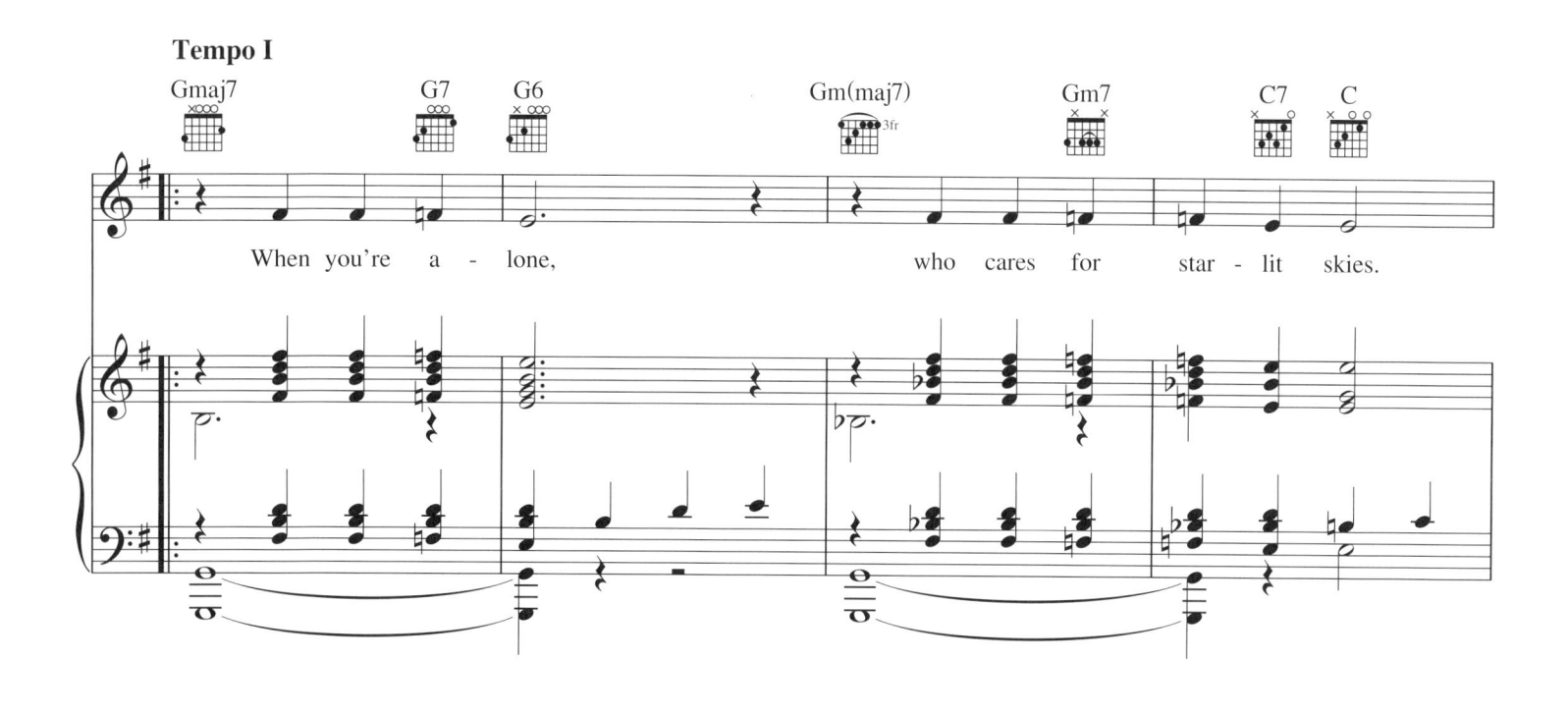

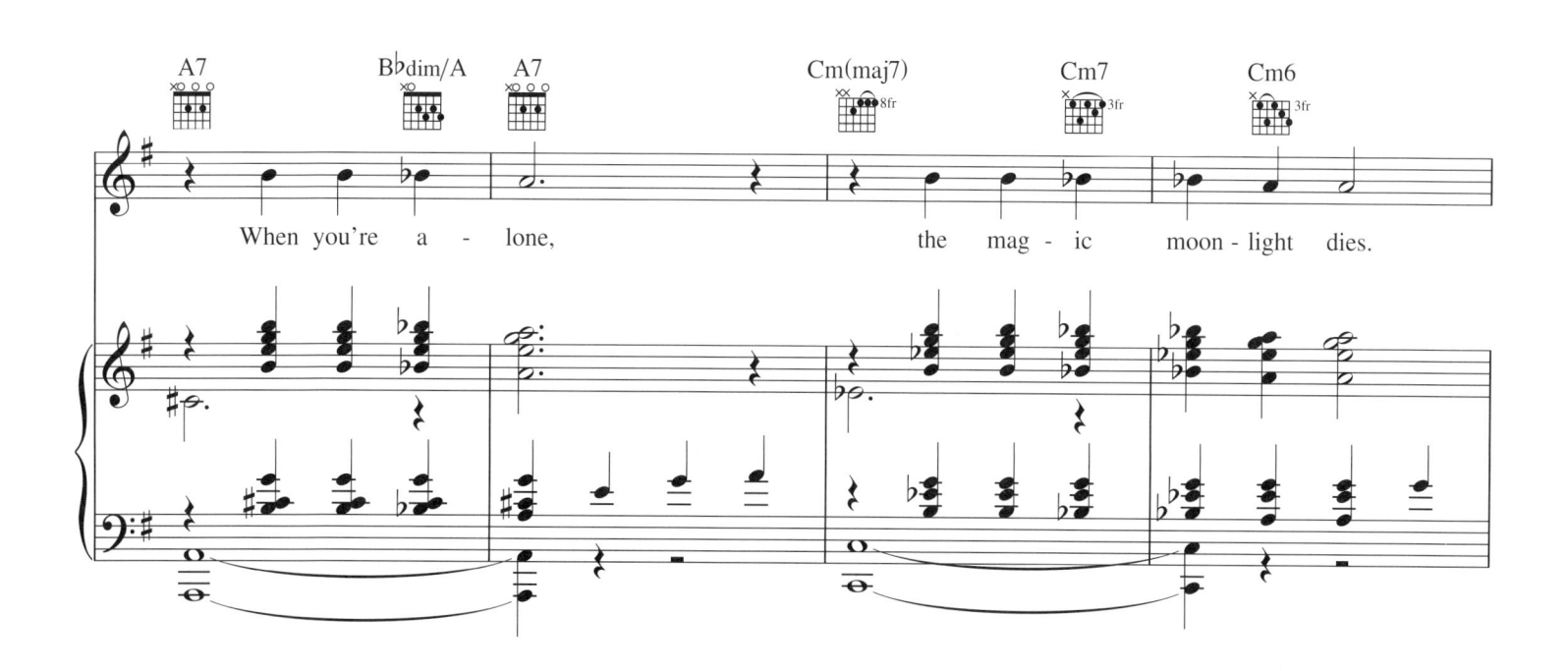

cov - er the heart-aches that ro - mance can bring.
per - ish and leave you with cas - tles in air.

Tempo I

When you're a - lone, who cares for star - lit skies.

When you're a - lone, the mag - ic moon - light dies.

G B7 Em C7 A7 A6 A7
At break of dawn there is no sun - rise,
G D7♯5 G A♭m6 D7 D+
when your lov - er has gone.
3
Gmaj7 G7 G6 Gm(maj7) Gm7 C7 C
What lone - ly hours the eve - ning shad - ows bring,
4fr
3fr

what lone-ly hours, with mem-'ries lin-ger-ing. Like fad-ed flow'rs, life can't mean an-y-thing, when your lov-er has gone. gone.

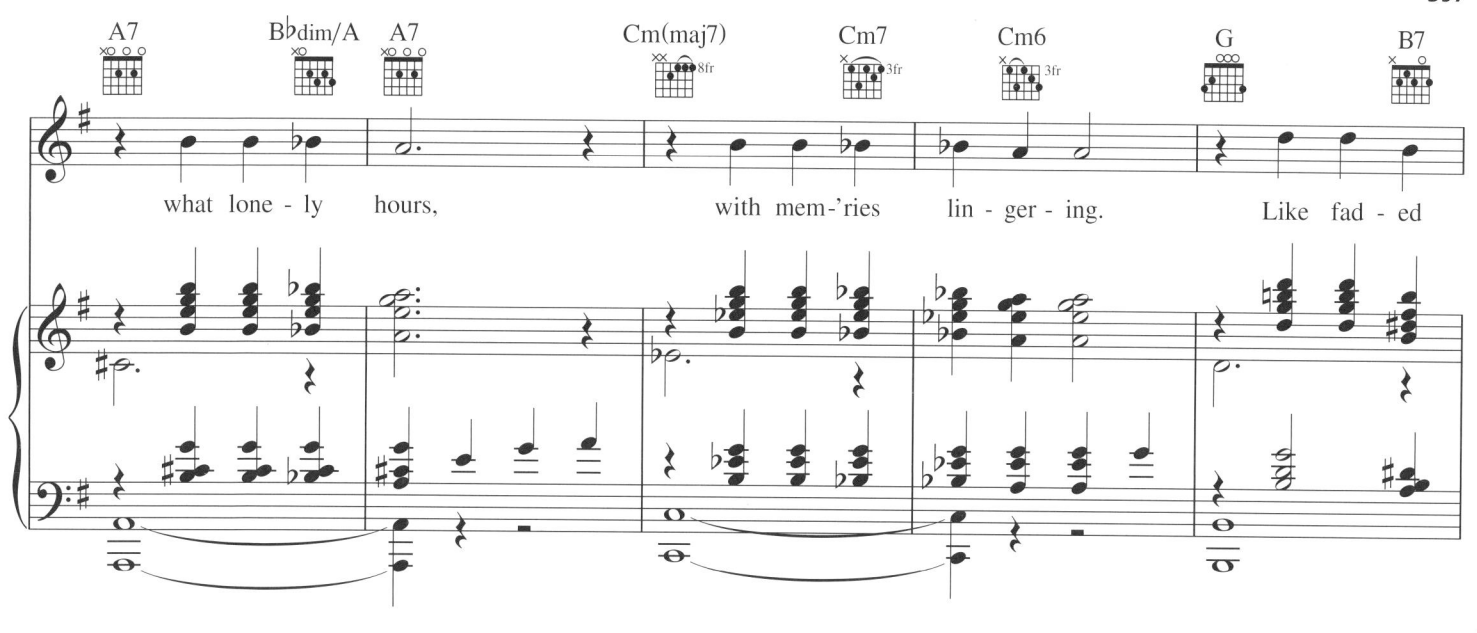

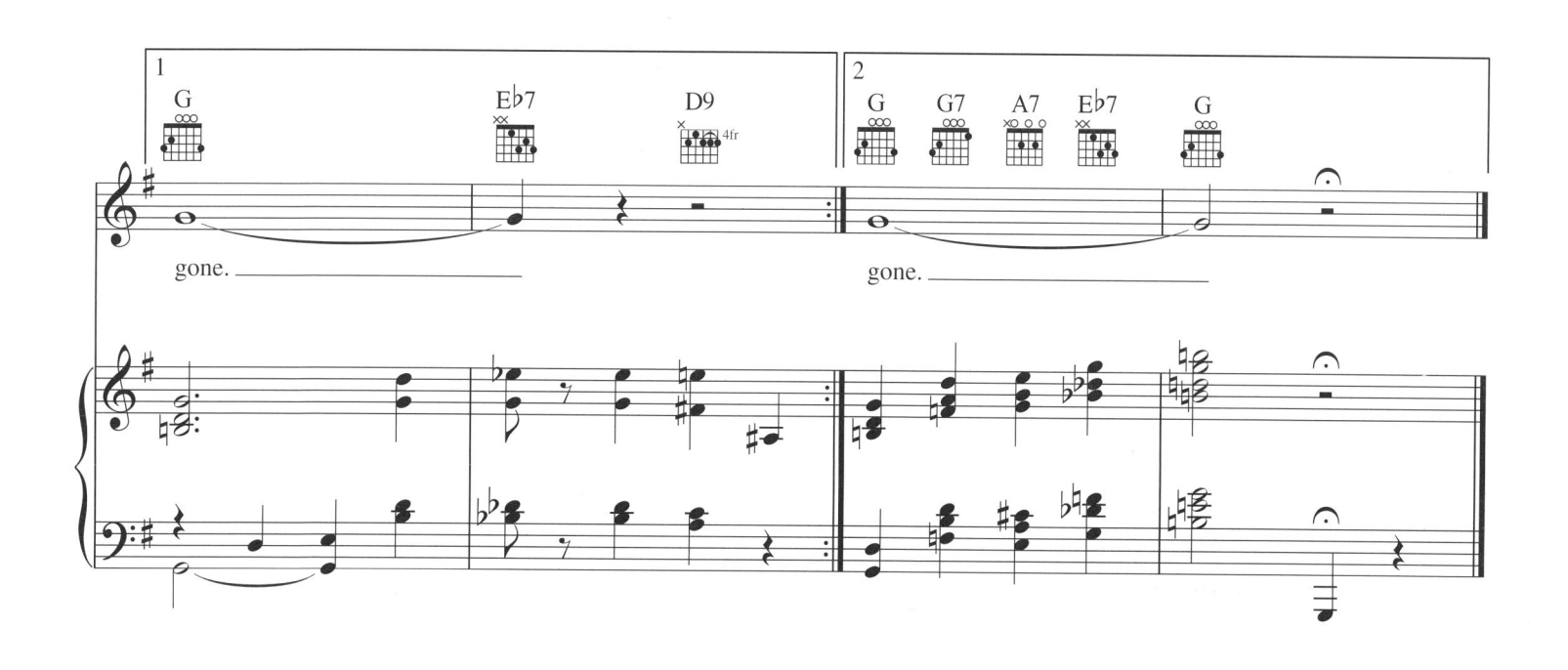

YOU MUST BELIEVE IN SPRING

Lyrics by ALAN and MARILYN BERGMAN
Music by MICHEL LEGRAND

Slowly, with feeling

When lonely feelings chill the meadows of your mind, just think, if winter come, can spring be far behind? Beneath the deepest snows, the secret of a rose is merely that it knows you

© 1967, 1968 (Copyrights Renewed) N.S. Beaujolais
All Rights Administered by EMI U CATALOG INC. (Publishing) and ALFRED MUSIC (Print)
All Rights Reserved Used by Permission

must be-lieve in spring! Just as a tree is sure its leaves will re-ap-pear, it knows its emp-ti-ness is just a time of year. The fro-zen moun-tain dreams of A-pril's melt-ing streams. How crys-tal clear it seems, you must be-lieve in spring! You must be-lieve in love and

| G7♭9/C | Cm | Cm7 | Fm7 | B♭7 |

trust it's on its way, just as the sleep-ing rose a-

| B♭7♭9/E♭ | E♭maj7 | Am7♭5 | D7♭9 |

waits the kiss of May. So in a world of snow,

| Gm7♭5 | C7♭9 | Fm7 | B♭7 |

of things that come and go, where what you think you know, you

| E♭maj7 | A♭maj7 | Dm7♭5 | G7 | Cm |

can't be cer-tain of, you must be-lieve in spring and love.